Highland
Clans and
Tartans

Highland Clans

and Tartans

R. W. Munro

CRESCENT BOOKS
NEW YORK

Contents

First English edition published in 1977 by
Octopus Books Limited,
59 Grosvenor Street, London W1

© MCMLXXVII Octopus Books Limited

This edition is published by Crescent Books,
a division of Crown Publishers, Inc.
One Park Avenue,
New York, N.Y. 10016

Produced by Mandarin Publishers Limited,
22a Westlands Road, Quarry Bay,
Hong Kong.

Printed in Hong Kong

Preface

The Highlands and Islands of Scotland have made a name for themselves throughout the world out of all proportion to their population or economic importance. The distinctive way of life of the Highland clans has been remembered long after the 'clan system' disappeared, and the aura of romance which still clings to them is undimmed by the centuries.

The reality, however, is often misrepresented, forgotten or unknown. On the one hand the days of the clans are looked back to as a golden age of pastoral peace or high-souled loyalty and courage, an idyllic and romantic picture which contrasts agreeably with our own more prosaic age; on the other hand they are made to appear as a black and dismal period of strife and plunder, hatred and revenge. Some believe that all traces of the clans were stamped out by a brutal and vindictive Government as the instrument of a despotic king; while others imagine that the true stream of Scottish clanship flows on untrammelled through its native hills into the twentieth century.

As so often happens, the truth really lies somewhere between the two extremes. I have tried in this book to describe the clans as they were in their heyday under the Stewart kings, to show how and why they collapsed in their old form, how some of their characteristics survived (or were at least revived), and how some of their old virtues – and perhaps even some of their old vices – have their influence on the Scottish people to this day.

In this revival one of the most remarkable features has been the growth in popularity of the tartan, and particularly the adoption of clan tartans and the world-wide association of Highland dress with the whole of Scotland.

It is no part of my purpose to exaggerate the distinction between Highland and Lowland Scotland, as I believe can be done. My viewpoint will not always be shared, therefore, by those who like to think in terms of an agelong feud between the Saxon and the Gaul.

In the final chapters I have told something of the work of modern clan societies of which little has been written. As one who has been in the movement for nearly forty years, and known some of its merits as well as some of its failings, I would dedicate these pages to the men and women throughout the world who seek through such societies to 'follow the fame of their ancestors', as the old proverb has it.

R. W. Munro

Note: As the spelling of names prefixed by Mac (= son) is largely a matter of custom or whim, it is hard to be completely consistent. Variations usually have little or no significance in determining the identity of an individual.

Where the part of the surname following the prefix is itself a proper name it is convenient, though not essential, to use a capital letter (e.g. MacDonald) otherwise to follow it with a smaller, or lower case, letter (e.g. Mackintosh or Macintosh = *Mac-an-toisich*, son of the Toisach; Maclean = *Mac-gille-Eoin*, son of the servant of John). When used purely as a patronymic form for the name of an individual (e.g. when the person's father was actually named Donald) the capital letter is certainly appropriate.

It is courteous to spell the name of living persons in the forms they themselves adopt, although some think the abridged 'Mc' or 'M'', much used in early records, are best avoided.

OPPOSITE This map of Scotland indicates the Highland area where the clans flourished. Land over 656 ft (200 m) is coloured brown. The so-called 'Highland Line' was not a regular frontier, but followed the edge of the mountains from about Dumbarton in the south-west to Dunnottar in the north-east. The low-lying coastal districts round the Moray Firth and elsewhere are also shown, as well as other features and some of the old district names

Prologue: Land and People

RIGHT The fortress of
Dunnottar overlooks the
North Sea where the foot-
hills of the Highlands
reach the east coast

That spectacular region of Scotland which
formed and fed the Highland clans is unique
in the British Isles. A great tableland has been
cut by nature into various mountain chains and
complexes, rising to 4000 feet above the sea and
divided by steep-sided valleys. Early writers
identify the high land running westwards
across Scotland from near the mouth of the
River Dee as 'The Mounth', a formidable
barrier between north and south; while the
backbone or spine of Scotland, stretching from
Ben Lomond northwards into Ross and Sutherland, was known as Drumalban, a watershed
from which short streams tumble down to the
deep sea-lochs of the west, and longer rivers
like the Tay and Spey flow more serenely to
the eastern coastal plains. Beyond the western
seaboard, lie two long strings of islands, the
Inner and Outer Hebrides, separated from
each other by the turbulent channel of the
Minch.

An eighteenth century military engineer
and surveyor wrote of 'that stupendous and
seemingly impenetrable barrier, which, like a
mighty wall, stretches along the southern
front of the Highlands'. Beginning not far
from the tall rock of Dumbarton, which rises
beside the waters of the Clyde, this barrier
circles the northern edge of the district of
Menteith, making it a borderland between
Highland and Lowland. Farther east the
River Forth 'bridled the wild Highlandman',
but the Highland peaks can be seen from the
castle rock of Stirling, where it has long been
bridged. Beyond the northern edge of the
fertile valley of Strathearn, and across Strathmore from the lesser Sidlaw and Ochil Hills,
the Grampian mountains 'seem to spring
suddenly from the low grounds at their base'.
Then the line turns north towards the sea at
Dunnottar, and circles back westward round
the foothills until it reaches the Moray
Firth somewhere beyond the mouth of the
River Spey.

Within this tenuous 'Highland line' lies
nearly one-fifth of the land area of Britain, and
nearly half of Scotland. For the most part it is
a mountain region, unsuited to the settled
agriculture on which a rural economy depends.
Much of it lies too high for permanent cultivation, and even on the lower ground the soils
are thin, intersected by rock and water, and
lacking in minerals. Hardier animals can find
summer pasture in plenty, but the arable
surface is sparse and scattered, and only a tiny
fraction has ever come under the plough.

Settlement tended to concentrate along the
eastern foothills, and in isolated pockets on

RIGHT The inauguration of Alexander III, from a fifteenth-century manuscript of Fordun's *Scotichronicon*, showing the Highlander hailing the king with the words 'Benach de Re Albanne Alexander macAlexander'. 'It must have astonished some contemporaries when the Highland bard hailed this Anglicised, French-speaking king as the descendant of Fergus I' (Prof. Gordon Donaldson, *Scottish Kings*)

BELOW In Lochindorb, a lonely Highland loch lying between the lands of Moray and Strathspey, are the remains of an island castle which was a stronghold of the lords of Badenoch. Not too remote to be captured and occupied by Edward I of England and his grandson Edward III, it became a useful basis for Robert II's unruly son, known as the 'Wolf of Badenoch'

the west coast and up the broader valleys leading into the interior. In a territory so much divided, the people living in each natural division led a life of their own. This encouraged the growth of a tribal system, where great families came to be established under their own patriarchal authority. This was part of 'the ancient Gaelic polity' (in the historian Macaulay's phrase) which Celtic immigrants brought with them from Ireland, and most of what we know of its early character is derived or deduced from Irish literary sources.

In the eleventh and twelfth centuries, under a series of active and powerful Scottish monarchs, the spread of feudalism produced a new social order in Scotland—'political military power in place of tribal authority, land held under contract instead of by tribal custom, the charter instead of the pedigree, the feudal superior in place of the head of the kin' (W. Mackay Mackenzie). The two orders met at the inauguration of Alexander III (1249), when an ancient Highland bard stepped forward and recited in Gaelic the genealogy of the 'Normanised' sovereign back to the shadowy founders of the royal line. The old ways were preserved longer in the Highlands and Islands than in the rest of Scotland, and by the fourteenth century the beginnings of many of

A mixture of Pictish, Scottish (or Irish) and Scandinavian ancestry went to the make-up of the clans. Among their forgotten forebears must be numbered the men who built the temple of standing stones at Callanish in Lewis (BELOW), crouched in subterranean wheel-houses and constructed the hill-forts which stud the Highland landscape. But in these prehistoric mists we find surer ground with the coming of St Columba, who made Iona a centre of Christianity and culture. A thirteenth-century 'Iona Psalter' (RIGHT), handwritten at Oxford with liturgical arrangements suitable for an Augustinian nun, gives prominence to Columba and his biographer Adomnan and may have belonged to a prioress of Iona

LORD OF ẙ ILLIS

FAR LEFT One of the great Christian monuments of Iona, standing near the entrance to the restored abbey church, is St Martin's Cross, carved from a solid block of Mull granite, fixed into a stepped pedestal and standing 14 ft (4.3 m.) high. Elaborately decorated on both faces, it probably dates from the early ninth century

Castle Sweⁿ LEFT, BELOW, believed to be the earliest stone castle in Scotland, stands on a high rock beside Loch Sween in Argyll. Its windowless walls, some 40 ft (12 m.) high and 7 ft (2 m.) thick, enclose an inner courtyard. Sweyn was a local ruler of Norse descent, whose family lost their lands before the Wars of Independence. In these wars Robert Bruce carried his fight for the throne into Argyll and defeated John MacDougall of Lorn in an ambush in the Pass of Brander RIGHT. The MacDonalds supported Bruce and as Lords of the Isles bore the galley on their shield LEFT, ABOVE

the clans which we can recognise today were already in existence. Some were gathered round the descendants of the old leaders of their race, while others were in process of formation whenever natural leaders of men appeared.

Strangely enough, though it was the wars of independence, 1296–1314, that united most of the nation, it was their aftermath that led to an unhappy division between Highland and Lowland Scotland which had previously been unknown. Exhaustion caused by the long struggle against English domination, and the weakness of the Crown's authority after the death of King Robert (Bruce) in 1329, led to a period of lawlessness and unrest. The process of unification was slowed down if not reversed, society was split up into separate groups under local leaders, and there was a 'sudden renaissance' of Gaelic power. A Lowland chronicler, who was the first to make the distinction between the 'wild' Scots, or Highlanders, and their 'tame' (or at least domesticated) neighbours to the south and east, found the former 'savage and untamed, rude and independent, given to rapine, ease-loving, of a docile and warm disposition, comely in person but unsightly in dress, hostile to the English people and language and (owing to diversity of speech) even to their own nation, and exceedingly cruel, but faithful and obedient to their king and country, and easily made to submit to law if properly governed'. It was not any special social structure, but the combative nature of the Highlanders that alarmed the Lowland observer.

Bruce's successors, including the first two Stewart kings, were not the men to ensure that the Highlands were 'properly governed'. An Act of Parliament of 1385, when the king's own son, Alexander, earl of Buchan was Justiciar of the North, alludes to many malefactors and 'caterans' found there; and it was that same Alexander, the so-called 'Wolf of Badenoch', who descended from his island lair in Lochindorb and with the aid of 'wyld wykked helandmen' burnt the towns of Forres and Elgin and gave the cathedral church of Moray to the flames. Two years later one of his sons was a ringleader when 300 or more Highlanders burst through the hills into Angus, and fought a battle in Glenisla in which the sheriff was killed. Parliament outlawed the offenders, and a list of them contains the first certain mention of a 'clan' in the north since the twelfth century. This 'Clanquhevil' (as the Lowland scribe called them) reappears four years later, with another unknown clan (usually rendered 'Kay') in that extraordinary 'ordeal by battle' on the North Inch of Perth, described by four fifteenth century writers and confirmed by official record, when two disputing clans sent 30 men each to fight it out before the king and his nobles, and 50 or more were slain.

As the fourteenth century drew to its close, the clans had definitely arrived on the national scene in Scotland. In the west a number of related groups were banded together under the banner of a Lord of the Isles, who twice brought the king's forces to battle early in the following century. A feudalized and more aggressive form of the old patriarchal system was emerging, and it is time to look at it more closely.

Who and What were the Clans?

The Gaelic word *clann* means children, and the central idea of clanship is kinship. A clan is a family and theoretically at least the chief is the father of it. Such a community structure was not peculiar to the Highlands and Islands, or even to Scotland, but in some form it survived there longer as a basis of society than in other places, and has left a memory of family loyalty and devotion which will for ever link the clans especially with the mountains and islands of the north and west.

It was undoubtedly the blood tie itself that held together the bulk of the people whose ancestors had inhabited a particular area from remote times. In theory the word clan should apply only to the family of the chief and the branches which could prove descent from him; the word has, however, been extended to embrace all those who acknowledged the authority of a chief and accepted his protection. Clans whose members are all descended from the same ancestor must be few; but if there are any they are likely to be found among the 'Macs' with an eponymous or name-father of whose 'native' origin no doubt has been expressed. Here it is impossible, or nearly so, to exclude those early Scots who may have come from Ireland. In clans like the MacGregors, Mackays, Mackenzies, Macnabs and Macneils, to name only a few, and also the Clan Donnachaidh (Robertsons) and the Rosses, it may well be that the chiefs and most of the clansmen share at any rate a Scottish, if not exactly a common, ancestry. In some of the northern clans, such as the Grants, Chisholms and Frasers, whose chiefs were probably all of Norman descent, there could not have been any tie of blood between the first chief and his people (except a few who may have arrived with him), although marriage with an heiress might have made it.

It was plainly of importance to have a man of bravery and good judgment as chief, but once the line was established the question of

who should be its leader was not often in dispute. Chiefship was not 'elective', but the old Celtic method of selecting an heir from a limited group of male kin lingered on in some clans. The Macleans bypassed the nearest heir in the reign of James IV, and so did the Clan-ranald in accepting John of Moidart as their chief – in both cases sanctioned by charters from the Crown. As feudal practice modified older customs, however, the automatic succession of an eldest son, or failing him the nearest male heir, became almost universal, with a 'Tutor' to lead the clan and administer his lands if a minor succeeded. Some restraint could still be brought to bear on the chief, as when 14 of the principal men of Clan Ross in 1577 exhorted the Laird of Balnagown to serve God, obey the Regent (Morton), and seek a remedy for the troubles which threatened, and advised him to consult with the heads of branch families (or cadets) lest he 'perish his hous kyn and freinds and tyne the riggis (lose the lands) that his fathers wan'.

It was not common, though not apparently forbidden, for an heiress to succeed to landed property, but it could be disastrous if clan leadership was involved. The lands of Calder (or Cawdor) and a great castle by the River

Nairn passed to a Campbell family by marriage with an heiress in 1510, and the name of Calder has shrunk to insignificance. An heiress succeeded to Ardnamurchan, and the Campbells eventually took over her lands, in spite of resistance by the male heirs which drove them to rebellion and final ruin. When MacLeod of Harris died in 1551 his daughter Mary succeeded: she was married to a Campbell, but in this case the struggle for power which followed left the MacLeods in possession.

The chief's younger sons and grandsons who founded families of their own were given part of the ancestral lands to maintain themselves. These cadet branches spread rapidly, and by frequent intermarriage both within the family group and outside it formed a complicated web of relationships which further strengthened the clan. It was a classless society although the degree of propinquity to the chief was not ignored in pride and precedence; the cadet whose family had come earliest from the main stem was usually a man of special importance, although furthest from the chief in actual blood relationship. Their common kinship, real or nominal, knit together every Highland community from the

BELOW The Isle of Mull and the lands around it, such as Morvern and Coll, were mainly Maclean territory. This seventeenth-century Blaeu map, from a survey by Timothy Pont, shows the castle of Duart perched on Mull's eastern promontory, with Loch-buie half-way along the south shore and Iona off the southern peninsula

chief to the humblest follower. Official records might speak of the earl of Argyll and the Lord of the Isles, Lord Lovat, or the Laird of Comar, and that was how they would be known in Edinburgh, but in their own country, and to all their clan, they were simply MacCailean *mor* (son of great Colin) or MacDhomnal (son of Donald), MacShimidh (son of Simon), or An Siosalach (The Chisholm).

Surnames are the hallmark of modern clans, but they were not in general use in the Highlands before the seventeenth century. The older system of patronymics persisted in the remoter areas, and is not yet quite abandoned.

name of their chief or a recognised variant of it; some took descriptive names or names of trades (such as Dow (= black), Roy (= red), Smith, Miller, Wright); and some apparently 'froze' their patronymic by using their father's name with the word 'Mac' before or 'son' after it. Such surnames, known as *sept* names, can thus correctly figure in the lists of followers of more than one clan, and unless a territorial link is known it is hard to identify the holder's clan. Another category of septs arose from smaller groups being linked with a large neighbour for physical protection in return for service, irrespective of any difference in origin

These of course changed with each generation, and (with the barbarous spelling which sometimes obscures their meaning) provide no clue to the clan to which the bearer belonged, although they often enshrine a pedigree of several generations. The earliest surviving rental of a Highland estate (1505) shows a multiplicity of 'Mac' names borne by tenants in Kintyre, but although they formed part of the great Clan Donald the name MacDonald does not appear once. Of two lists of inhabitants in the Grant country of Strathspey, dated 1537 and 1569, the first (drawn up locally) contains 71 names in patronymic form, while the other (written in Edinburgh) has 40 names all with the surname Grant.

When surnames were adopted, it was natural that a nominal kinship with the ruling family should be established. Some families took the

or surname.

A clan can therefore be seen as a variable unit, consisting not so much of people with the same surname as of those who followed the same chief. In early records a common description might include the chief with his 'kin, friends, servants, assisters and parttakers', and although less romantic that would get near the truth. A telling phrase which found its way into a notable Act of Parliament, embracing those united 'be pretence of blude or place of thair duelling', neatly enshrines the combination of genuine and nominal family ties and territorial neighbourhood which was basic to the make-up of the clans.

The territorial link was important, and became more so, because the feudal system, introduced among the clans by deliberate royal policy, was based on land-holding. The lands

The proud castles of the island chiefs probably developed from early forts or 'duns' built as places of refuge and defence and often rising on bold rocks near the sea shore. Dunvegan castle BELOW built by the MacLeods over many centuries, includes an early curtain wall, an ancient keep (seen left, below modern tower) and sixteenth-century house. Until after 1745, the only access was by sea gate through the curtain wall and along a narrow entrance passage OPPOSITE, BELOW

on which a clan was settled were bestowed on individuals, and there was at least no formal recognition of any 'tribal land' or 'clan territories'. Modern 'clan maps' indicate the areas where different names were mainly found: these were not usually owned or peopled exclusively by the clan in question, but were rather 'spheres of influence' where a chief's authority was acknowledged, and consequently they were changing from time to time and merging at many points. Yet Kintail to a Mackenzie, Mull to a Maclean, and Loch Eil to a Cameron, is still his own 'clan country'.

By feudal theory the king was regarded as owning all the land in the kingdom, which he divided among his most important followers. Each of these followers received a formal written charter, giving him legal rights over his part of the land in return for certain obligations to the king, and these charter holders could then divide their estates among dependants in return for similar support. In the clans the blood-tie was fortified by two forms of tenure peculiar to Scotland, the *wadset* and the *feu*, both in practice heritable and so giving their holders the security of tenure necessary for establishing a 'landed' family. The cadets, who were usually *wad-*

setters, granted long-term *feus* or *tacks* to others, who in turn gave short-term leases to their tenants, some of whom might be connected either by descent or marriage.

There was every advantage in the chief of a clan holding his lands by charter, but if he rebelled against the king he automatically forfeited his position as feudal 'superior' or territorial overlord, and the lands reverted to the crown and were granted to someone else. This could lead to trouble, for a clansman would usually continue to follow his own chief whether or not he were still the superior. Another source of divided loyalty arose when a chief who held his land from a great lord was forced to accept him as a feudal superior rather than holding direct from the crown. The chief and the superior might take opposite sides in a dispute, or a chief might hold two parts of his land from different superiors who quarrelled. In Lochaber, successive chiefs of Mackintosh received charters of lands occupied mainly by Camerons and MacDonalds, who resented his position and preferred to obey their own chiefs, Lochiel and Keppoch. Further north, Mackintosh's own clan country lay partly within Huntly's lordship of Badenoch, and the clan-feudal clash was the root cause of a long feud. Some of these

ABOVE Duart castle overlooks the Sound of Mull, one of the great sea lanes of the Hebrides. It was restored and modernised 60 years ago by Sir Fitzroy Maclean of Duart who lived to be a centenarian and the chief's flag flies when his grandson, Lord Maclean, is at home

1

2

Map showing the location of some of the principal castles of the clan chiefs, identifying by surname those who occupied them about the time of James VI (1566–1625). Where a name is attached to more than one castle, one was usually the seat of the chief while the head of a subsidiary clan or family lived in the other.

Of these four great castles, Kisimul (1) has been restored by Macneil of Barra, and the other three are splendid even in decay: Castle Tioram (2), on a tidal island in Loch Moidart, was home of MacDonald of Clanranald; Inchconnel or Innis Chonnell (3) in Loch Awe passed from the Mac-Dougalls to the Campbells in the fourteenth century, and was their chief residence until succeeded by Inveraray; and Invergarry castle (4), on Creag an Fhithich or Raven's Rock above Loch Oich, was the seat of MacDonell of Glengarry

3

4

Brove
Mackay

Tongue
Mackay

Stornoway
MacLeod

Ardvreck
MacLeod

Dunrobin
Sutherland

Balnagown
Ross

Foulis
Munro

Cromarty
Urquhart

Duffus
Sutherland

Duntulm
MacDonald

Darnaway *Stewart*

Leod
Mackenzie

Kilravock
Rose

Altyre
Cumming

Borve
MacDonald

Dunvegan
MacLeod

Strome
MacDonald

Erchless
Chisholm

Dounie
Fraser

Cawdor
Campbell

Huntly
Gordon

Moy
*Mackintosh
& Clan Chattan*

Urquhart
Grant

Freuchie
Grant

Dunakin
MacKinnon

Eilean Donan
Mackenzie

Dunskaith
MacDonald

Invergarry
MacDonald

Cluny
Macpherson

isimul
Macneil

Tioram
MacDonald

Achnacarry
Cameron

Struan
Robertson

Blair
Murray

Mingary
MacIan

Dunara
MacKinnon

Stalker
Stewart

Menzies
Menzies

Breachacha
Maclean

Duart
Maclean

Dunstaffnage
Campbell

Eilean Ran
Macnab

Finlarig
Campbell

Dunollie
MacDougall

Kilchurn
Campbell

Moy
Maclean

Inchconnel
Campbell

Inveraray
Campbell

Arrochar
MacFarlane

Doune
Stewart

Dunevin
Macfie

Lachlan
MacLachlan

Rossdhu
Colquhoun

Inveryne
Lamont

Skipness
Campbell

Dunivaig
MacDonald

competing interests were fomented by those (sometimes the government itself), who wished to set one clan against another and the problem of maintaining law and order was complicated by the existence of many 'broken clans', that is clansmen living under a superior who was not also their chief. The MacGregors, to whom reference will be made later, are the best-known example.

No title to possession, however legal, was worth anything without armed force to back it, and it was in the interests of a chief to have as many followers as he could effectively muster. Stories are told of various clans whose chiefs 'enticed' outsiders into the clan, and even allowed if not encouraged them to assume the name itself. Besides the Lordship of the Isles, embracing Clan Donald and many others, the great confederacy of Clan Chattan came into being chiefly for mutual defence and protection. Sometimes it happened that members of a clan who had moved from their original home attached themselves to the chief of the locality where they settled, like the Macleans of Dochgarroch near Inverness who were linked with Clan Chattan and separated by the breadth of Scotland from their chief in Mull; but it is on record that a group of Maclean tenants in Strathglass, when accused of witchcraft in 1662, appealed to Maclean of Duart and had their case tried outside the Chisholm jurisdiction. Burghs were well aware, too, of the dangers inherent in their burgesses owing loyalty to chiefs whose interests might not coincide with those of a merchant community, and in 1556 Inverness forbade 'the intakyn of clannit men and strangeris'.

To defend themselves from attack, and no doubt also to impress their neighbours and even their own clan, many of the chiefs built strong castles at key points in their territories. Often these would be on the site of an earlier fort, such probably as Dunvegan of the MacLeods, Dunollie of the MacDougalls, and Dundoward (later Duart) of the Macleans. Some chose a rocky islet in the sea, such as Kisimul in Barra of the MacNeils and Mackenzie's castle of Eilean Donan in Kintail,

22

and it is known that Dunvegan's only access until after 1745 was by the sea. The Clan Donald had a whole series of castles, from the Lord of the Isles' island 'palace' in Loch Finlaggan and his seaboard castles of Ardtornish and Aros, to the branch clans' Dunscaith and Duntulm in Skye (MacDonalds of Sleat), Castle Tioram in Moidart (Clanranald), and Invergarry on Loch Oich (Glengarry). Besides Inveraray, which is relatively modern, the Campbells had Kilchurn and Inchconnel on Loch Awe when it was to their advantage to be a 'far cry' from the centres of authority.

Each clan would also have its accepted gathering ground as a rendezvous in time of war and also for peaceful meetings. No doubt some of the larger clans had more than one, even if the exact sites are for the most part unrecorded and forgotten. To regulate the affairs of the Fraser lordship of Lovat and settle a tutor during the chief's minority, 300 'leading men of the name' were convened near a ford on the River Beauly in 1577; at other times they met at Tomnahurich, the fairy hill at Inverness now used as a cemetery, chosen as a 'mediat place' for the muster of men from the Aird, Stratherrick and Abertarff for the campaign which ended at Worcester. The scattered tribes of Clan Chattan met in

1609 at Termit in Petty, near Inverness, to proclaim their loyalty to young Lachlan Mackintosh of Dunachton, then a minor. A long ridge at Ballintomb in the heart of Strathspey, where three standing stones mark a site of ancient importance near the point where the Dulnain enters the Spey, became the 'ordinary place of rendezvous' of the Grants, and remained for long a scene of trial and punishment. Loch Sloy and Ben Cruachan were so well known to the Mac-Farlanes and the Campbells that they shouted them as battle slogans.

As feudal ways penetrated the Highlands, the chief's patriarchal sway was buttressed by personal powers delegated by the crown, for which the elders of the clan could hardly call him to account. In the various parts of the Lordship of the Isles there were *brieves* or professional Gaelic judges, with a right of appeal to the council at Finlaggan in Islay. But in the lesser clans it was the chief in person, or as represented by his bailie, who administered justice. The records of baron courts which have survived show not only the punishment of malefactors but the regulation of a multitude of everyday concerns, often with the advice and consent of 'the whole commons and tenants'. These might range, as we learn from the

Breadalbane papers (early seventeenth century), from laying down that all stock should be kept at the mountain 'shealings' between 8 June and 15 July, in order to rejuvenate the lower pasture land, to punishing wives found drinking in the public brew-house without their husbands. It was a pastoral society, with an economy based mainly on cattle; only the simplest methods of cultivation were in vogue, and the larger fields were held in common and divided into strips on the old 'runrig' system. Stock and seed corn as well as the land to grow it on were often provided by the chief, and it was common practice for the tenants' rents in bad years to be remitted and grain supplied in times of famine.

The Highland area was still extensively afforested, though the rest of Scotland was already losing its trees. Timber had acquired a commercial value, and unsupervised cutting and damage was discouraged. Hunting and other outdoor sports had an important place in the life of the clans, and were a popular way of entertaining visitors. The Fraser chronicles tell of deer drives lasting for several days among the hills. Queen Mary was present at a great hunt in the forest of Mar, and a seventeenth century powder horn depicts a Highland chief with dirk and musket, his huntsman carrying

One of the warrior effigies OPPOSITE, LEFT found in West Highland church-yards dating from about 1350–1550, shows Bricius MacFingone, a MacKinnon chief buried in Iona, wearing a pointed bascinet or light helmet, coif or tippet of mail, and quilted tunic reaching to his knees (of a kind sometimes mistaken for a kilt, as the padding is in vertical strips). In a water-colour, dated *c.* 1570, a Scottish Highlander OPPOSITE, RIGHT is dressed in a diagonally striped jacket belted at the waist, short pants or trews, and a long mantle. Decoration on a seventeenth-century powder horn ABOVE depicts a hunting scene with a Highland laird, musket on shoulder and dog on leash, and a companion blowing a horn and carrying a musket-rest

a musket-rest and a dog on leash. A martial as well as a social purpose was served by making these hunts the occasion also of contests in archery, shooting with firelocks, fencing with cudgels, running, jumping, swimming, throwing the bar, and all kinds of manly exercises.

The ordinary dress of the clans can be guessed at from a few written descriptions, as the dramatic stone effigies of the West Highlands may be presumed to show only the chiefs accoutred for war. From Abbot Bower's account of how Alexander of the Isles appeared before James I *'camisia et femoribus tantum indutus'*, it has been thought that he wore a plaid with his legs and arms bare (his own 'romantic national costume', as Andrew Lang observed, though others had translated it less romantically as his shirt and drawers). John Major, historian and philosopher, wrote in 1521 of the 'wild Scots' having no covering for the leg from the middle of the thigh to the foot, and wearing a mantle (*chlamyde*) instead of an upper garment and a shirt dyed with saffron. James V seems to have been partial to Highland customs, and in the Treasurer's accounts for 1538 there is mention of a short Highland jacket of velvet 'for the king's grace', tartan hose or trews (here 'tartan' probably referred to material, and not to colour or pattern), and a long Highland

ABOVE Sir Duncan Campbell of Glenorchy, during whose vigorous and methodical administration the family estates were extended and improved, had this portrait of himself painted in 1619. The castles of Eilean Donan OPPOSITE at the mouth of Loch Duich and Strome LEFT at the mouth of Loch Carron commanded the narrow seas between the mainland and Skye and were reckoned to be 'richt necessar for the danting of the Isles'. The former has been restored, the latter is in ruins

shirt. An astonished French visitor in 1549 wrote: 'They wear no clothes except their dyed shirts and a sort of light woollen covering (*couverture*) of several colours' – presumably the plaid described by Bishop Leslie (1578) as 'long and flowing but capable of being neatly gathered up at pleasure into folds'.

George Buchanan's account of 1582 states that the Highlanders – or his remarks may be confined to the Islanders – 'delight in variegated garments, especially stripes, and their favourite colours are purple and blue', although for camouflage in the heather they preferred a dark brown. Their ancestors wore plaids of many colours (*sagis versicoloribus plurifariam*), wrapped in which they could brave the severest storms and lie down to sleep even in the midst of snow. An Irish account of the Hebridean levies sent to Ulster in 1594 says they were distinguished from Irish soldiers by their arms and clothing, habits and language, 'for their exterior dress was mottled cloaks of many colours (*breachhrait ioldathaca*) with a fringe to their shins and calves, their belts were over their loins outside their cloaks' – surely an early reference to the belted plaid which was the precursor of the modern kilt.

In the support of a large number of clansmen, the chief had an armed force on which he could call at all times. It would have been usurpation for anyone else to presume to their command (unless during his minority or incapacity), so he was the hereditary colonel, and the heads of cadet houses were the natural officers of the clan 'regiments'. Estimates of the number of fighting men which could be raised at various times range from 4000 by the Campbells of Argyll and 3000 by the Mackenzies, down to between 100 and 200 men by small clans like the Mackinnons and the Chisholms. MacDonell of Keppoch, asked the amount of his income, is said to have replied 'I can call out and command 500 men'. Highland warfare could be a bloody business, with terrible wounds. According to the clan chronicles, only half a dozen Frasers who fought at the 'field of the shirts' in 1544 survived out of 300, and 280 Macleans (including 80 of their chief men) were killed in Islay in 1598. In a bloody skirmish at the back of Ben Wyvis between the Munros and some western clans the dead included 11 members of the chief's family who were to succeed one after another, 'so that the succession of Foulis fell unto a chyld then lying in his cradle'.

It would be a mistake to accept unreservedly the Lowlander's belief in the ferocity and cruelty of the Highlanders, although some

Magnificent sculptured panels ABOVE embellish a canopied recess over the tomb at Rodel of Alexander MacLeod of Harris and Dunvegan, prepared by him in 1528, nearly 20 years before he died. At the ends of the upper series are a castle with two towers and a galley under sail (both part of the old MacLeod arms) with between them panels showing the Madonna and Child flanked by two episcopal figures; the lower series shows a deer hunt (details, OPPOSITE, LEFT) with several figures, dogs, and three noble stags; St Michael and Satan busy at the weighing of souls; and finally a Latin inscription clearly identifying the chief commemorated and the date

RIGHT The artist R. R. McIan drew this vigorous impression of the Lord of the Isles delivering judgment on the Council Isle in Loch Finlaggan, Islay BELOW The sculptured monuments of the West Highlands are elaborately ornamented. Some of the favourite themes appear on these specimens preserved at Kilmory of Knap in Mid Argyll, including long-shafted crosses with decorative heads, great two-handed swords or claymores, galleys, mythical beasts and interlacing foliage

ugly tales of massacre sully the pages of the clan chronicles. Some of the worst atrocities were sanctioned by a 'commission of fire and sword' from the king himself, and feuds which ruined whole communities and countrysides could have their origin in simple factors like the pressure of population on inadequate resources. Disputes and alliances between kindred were undoubtedly the cause of others, or the simple desire to plunder the richer low country which clans on the Highland fringe firmly believed had once belonged to their ancestors. There is a sense of economic reality, however, in the provision, known from a sixteenth century account of the Hebrides, that 'no labourers of the ground were permitted to stir forth of the country whatever their master might have ado except only gentlemen which labour not, that the labour belonging to the tilling of the ground and winning of their corns may not be left undone'.

For the passage of light armed forces, the sea formed a convenient highway on the west, and the mountains were seamed with glens and passes. The Great Glen was the most important, while others linked Badenoch with Moray, Atholl and Lochaber, Deeside and Atholl with Strathmore, and Argyll with the Lowland valleys and plains.

Where communication was always by sea, fighting usually consisted of coastal raids, although there were some larger expeditions. Bruce is said to have warned his successors that the islanders, in vessels well adapted to their coasts (even if others might think them awkward) could do extensive damage to an enemy unfamiliar with sea warfare with little hurt to themselves. 'Hieland galeyis' is a term often used in early accounts of the Hebrides: according to a seventeenth century official report to the Privy Council, the galley was a vessel with 16 to 24 oars, and a 'birlinn' had 12 to 16 oars, their war-time crews numbering three men to each oar. A written agreement shows that in 1354 John of Lorn (MacDougall) was allowed by John of the Isles (MacDonald) to build eight vessels of 12 or 16 oars each, and by a royal charter of 1498 Alasdair MacLeod of Dunvegan undertook to maintain one 26-oar and two 16-oar galleys for the service of the crown. The maintenance of seaboard castles must have required regular transport of supplies, and in 1503 when the island chiefs rebelled against James IV, bases at Eilean Donan and Strome in Wester Ross were reckoned 'richt necessar for the danting [daunting] of the Isles'.

There is no reason, however, to suppose that the lighter side of daily life was neglected by the clans. The stone carvings found in many parts of the West Highlands are proof, with their elaborate tracery and lively scenes, of an artistic talent fostered under the Lordship of the Isles. Highland harps still exist dating from at least the sixteenth century, and families of hereditary harpers were known. The bagpipe is of great antiquity (Scotland lays no claim to its invention), and its music went well with the outdoor life of mountain and glen, as it did for keeping the rowers' time when crossing the broader sea passages like the Minch between Skye and Harris. The Highlanders' development of the bagpipe as an inspiring instrument of war seems to have come during the sixteenth century, and the MacCrimmons, hereditary pipers to MacLeod, are credited with evolving the *ceol mor* or *piobaireachd* (pibroch), the classical music of the Highland bagpipe. Training 'colleges' for pipers from all parts were maintained by the MacLeods and MacDonalds in Skye, taught by the MacCrimmons and MacArthurs, and by the Macleans in Mull. Nor was other professional learning despised, for several Highland clans included families with the hereditary role of serving the chiefs and their families in the art of medicine. Medical treatises were translated into Gaelic, and one of them (said

to have cost as much as 60 milch cows) was so precious that when the doctor crossed an arm of the sea the book was sent round by land.

Formal education was of course in the hands of the church from the earliest times. When Aberdeen University was founded in 1495 those who dwelt in the mountains and on the west coast were said to be 'rude and ignorant of letters'. The first Scottish 'education act' a year later, providing that eldest sons of barons and freeholders were to attend grammar school and learn the art of law, may have been no more than a statement of intent; but during the century which followed there are references to grammar schools at Dunkeld, Inverness, Fortrose and Tain. The sons of Fraser, Mackenzie, Munro and Ross chiefs were educated at Beauly and Kinloss (in the 'low country'), and three cultured clerics in the Isles wrote devotional, topographical and poetic works on the eve of the Reformation.

The bards' main job was to extol the chief and his ancestors, and to produce and perpetuate the story of the clan's achievements and victories. They vied with each other in tracing the line back to an heroic founder, through a long and mythical pedigree, and to suit changing fashions they might fix its origin on an Irish princeling, a Scottish king, or even a Roman pope. These professional poets who were a part of every chief's household were also the guardians and transmitters of the great Gaelic tales which were to survive long after the clan era, to be picked up as remnants, woven into epic form in the eighteenth century, and recorded more scientifically as folklore in the nineteenth and twentieth. In some cases the chronicle and the pedigree were combined and eventually written down: the oldest of these date only from the seventeenth century (though acknowledging earlier sources), like the history of the Mackintoshes in English and Latin, the Gaelic histories of Clan Donald in the 'Red and Black Books of Clanranald' and the Fraser chronicles in English by the minister of Wardlaw.

While such tales inevitably fed the vainglory of both chief and followers, they also, for us, enlarge upon the sober evidence of contemporary written records, which are all too scanty in many Highland families. Yet in spite of all the hazards to which they were exposed, charters signed and sealed by the Lords of the Isles (including the sole surviving Gaelic charter, granting lands in Islay in 1408), and many other documents which tell us of land and social customs, have been preserved. Between the feudal record completed at the time, and the bardic chronicle later committed to writing,

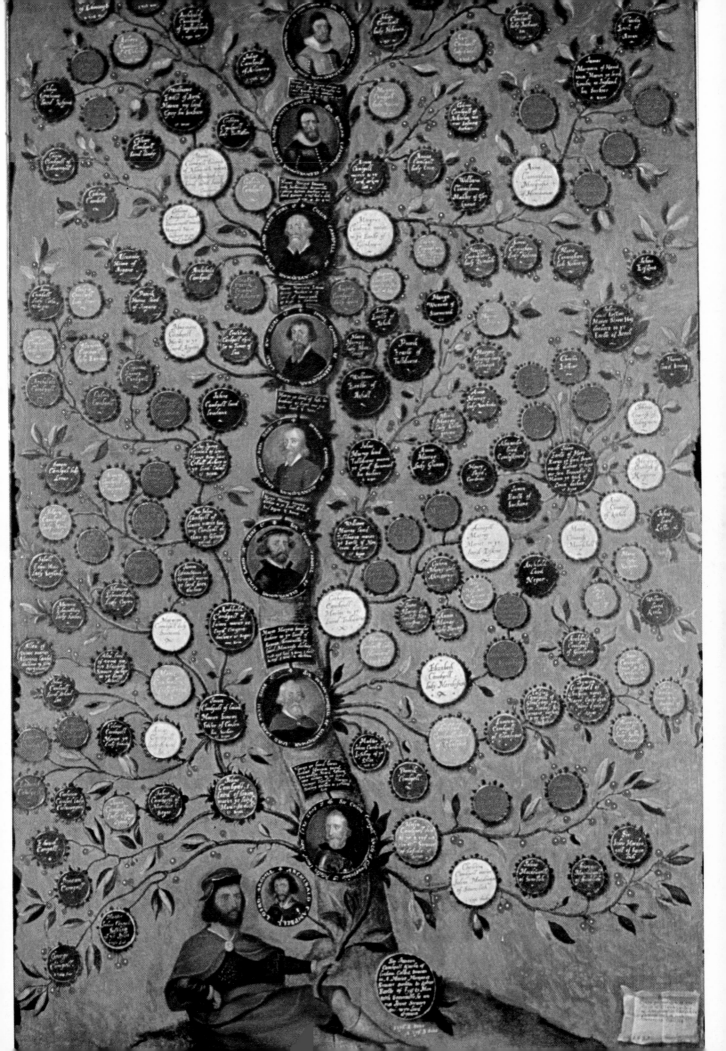

RIGHT The music of the clarsach or Highland harp must have accompanied the singing and added to the gaiety or pathos of many family gatherings. The harper was an important member of a chief's household and two of the oldest surviving instruments are associated with the Robertsons. The Lude harp shown here, said to have come to the family from Queen Mary, is only 31 ins (78 cm.) high and beautifully decorated. On the box and comb the designs are mainly geometrical, but the bow is carved with scrolls, leaves and monsters in typically Celtic style

we can glimpse from within something of life as it was lived in the heyday of the clans.

No general account of the clans, however incomplete, can afford to ignore their impact on the rest of Scotland, and particularly on the central government. After a succession of weak monarchies and a prolonged regency, James I returned to his kingdom in 1424 from a long imprisonment in England determined (in the graphic phrase preserved by the chronicler) to 'make the key keep the castle and the bracken-bush the cow'. After dealing with his powerful Albany cousins, the family who had ruled Scotland in his absence, (the Lord of the Isles was one of the jury who convicted them) he began by ordering the lords who had lands 'beyond the Mounth' to repair their castles and live there 'for the gracious government of the lands by good policing', and by closing an escape route to Ireland by placing restrictions on contact by sea.

Signs that he meant to reckon with the clans can be read into James's descent on Inverness in 1428: he summoned a number of chiefs to meet him there, seized them and executed three of them. He later released several after a short imprisonment, took the Lord of the Isles into his own household, and showed a conciliatory attitude to some clan groups by

freeing them from the legal penalties for past killings and robberies. The king may not have made much lasting impression on the Highlands, but when one of his murderers escaped into Atholl he was caught by 'Robert Duncansone of Strowane' (chief of the Robertsons or Clan Donnachaidh) whose lands were made a barony by James II as a reward.

Just as in the Borders – where clans and 'clannit men' were also to the fore – the Wardens of the Marches had for long been held responsible for law and order, so in the Highlands in 1475 James III began the policy of appointing Lieutenants for the same purpose. When Argyll and Huntly were thus employed, their followers, the Campbells and the Gordons had a chance to become trained soldiers and work off their surplus energy, at least nominally, on 'the king's business'. With no standing army or police force, it was convenient to send a powerful noble or clan chief with an adequate following to crush rebellion and enforce the law, even if there was a risk that he might advance his own interests and pay off old scores in doing so. One of the rebels dealt with was the Lord of the Isles himself, who had entered into a secret treaty with England. The final extinction of the Lordship in 1493 was undertaken by James IV, who went to the West

Highlands and Hebrides in person to receive the submission of its tributary chiefs, many of whom received crown charters of their lands.

The clans were now at the peak of their influence, with many lesser chiefs in the west and north free to provide for their own expansion. They were also recognized as political units by the crown – the Stewarts were after all a great family federation themselves, who well understood the bond between chief and clan: and national politics had not yet intervened to set one group of clans against another. In 1496 the island chiefs were made answerable for the arrest and punishment of offenders belonging to their own clans, under penalty of being made liable themselves for any claims by those who had been injured. Various attempts to restore the Lordship were made, and one led by the grandson of the last Lord took three years to suppress: but royal authority was eventually restored, and the king had an unusually large Highland contingent in the army which he led against the English at Flodden.

James V was responsible for a savage 'commission of fire and sword' (an instrument which was to become all too familiar) granted in 1528 to his half-brother James earl of Moray for punishing the Clan Chattan for

It is not easy to visualise the inside of a Highland castle as it used to be, but some idea may be obtained from the Long Gallery at Crathes OPPOSITE, BELOW on lower Deeside, completed in the 1590s for a long-descended baronial family. The oak ceiling and panelling are unusual and some of the furniture belongs to a later period. The painted ceiling BELOW in another room is contemporary with the castle

VIRTUTIS · GLORIA · MERCES

GARG 'N UAIR DHUISGEAR

widespread disorders in Badenoch and else-where. The order was not carried out to the last letter, but it demanded the 'utter ex-termination and destruction' of the clan and its supporters, leaving none alive but priests, women and bairns – the latter to be shipped across the North Sea to the Low Countries or Norway. In the Isles, however, the king used some of the chiefs as his agents and made personal visits, culminating in a great naval 'progress' in 1540 from which he brought home a handsome 'bag' of captives (Mackay, Mac-Leod, Mackenzie, MacDonald, Maclean and probably Macneil). In Queen Mary's brief reign the most important event was the Reformation of the Church, which left the old lands of Beauly priory in Fraser hands, Iona went to the Macleans, and the Mackenzies acquired the Chanonry of Ross.

With James VI of Scotland we reach the high-water mark of royal concern in Highland affairs. Best known as the protagonist of the divine right of kings, he was notable also for his determination to end the feuds which tore his kingdom apart, and for trying in some novel ways to bring peace and 'civilitie' to problem areas such as the Highlands and Islands and the borders. Feudal magnates were already answerable for their dependants' good be-haviour, but James decided to extend and adapt the Border practice of getting the lairds to sign *bands* (or bonds) to keep the peace and obey the royal authority, under stated penalties, and to accept responsibility for their whole family and clan as well as for their tenants. In 1587, a few months after he had reached the the age of 21 and assumed full authority, Parliament passed an Act which was a clear

34

recognition of the power of the clan system. It was designed to enforce the law and to ensure that where the chief rather than the superior held the real power it would be his duty to arrest and hand over any offenders of his own clan, and make reparation to the injured party. Appended to the Act were two rolls of names – the first listing 105 landlords and bailies in the Highlands and Islands where 'broken men hes duelt or presentlie duellis', and the other listing 34 clans in the same area who lived on the lands of various landlords but depended on the 'directionis' of their own captains, chiefs and chieftains and principals of branches although 'oftymes aganis the willis of thair landlordis' (besides 22 and 17 respectively in the Borders, to which the Act also applied). One of the first duties of a special committee of the Privy Council set up under Chancellor

Maitland of Thirlestane was to secure the agreement of all landlords throughout the kingdom to a new 'General Band' pledging themselves to be responsible for the good behaviour of their tenants and adherents: but the list of those in the Highlands who found sureties is so small in comparison with the full list that it seems only to have touched the fringe of the problem.

The king was convinced that disorder in the Highlands and Islands was robbing him of revenue enjoyed by his ancestors. In 1597, on the pretext that rents and services were not being paid, all landlords, chieftains and leaders of clans were ordered to produce their titles by the middle of May 1598 and to find sureties for regular payment and observance of law and order – failure to do so could mean forfeiture of all rights, real or pretended. Few records

ABOVE Chronicles handed down in hereditary bardic families such as the MacVurichs were being written down by the seventeenth century. The Red and Black Books of Clanranald lie open at a poetical Gaelic description of the clans joined in the array of the last Lord of the Isles (right) and the traditional genealogies of several Highland families (left) survive to show who complied and who did not, but the upshot was that the MacLeod territories of Lewis and Harris, and the lands of Dunvegan and Glenelg, were declared to be at the king's disposal. Rory *mor*, the powerful chief of Dunvegan (whose titles were unchallengeable), managed to save his estates by personal appeals to James: but Lewis became the victim of a violent experiment in 'colonisation' by Lowlanders from Fife which only added to the islanders' miseries, did nothing to help the royal finances, and was eventually abandoned. The king's attitude to his Highland subjects is plain enough from what he himself wrote (*Basilicon Doron*, published 1599/1603):-

'As for the Hielands, I shortly comprehend them all in two sorts of people: the one, that dwelleth in our main land that are barbarous, and yet mixed with some show of civilitie: the other that dwelleth in the Isles and are all utterlie barbarous, without any sort or show of civilitie. For the first sort (he advised his son and heir), put straitly in execution the laws made already by me against their overlords and the chiefs of their clans, and it will be no difficultie to danton them. As for the other sort, think no other of them all than of wolves and wild boars; and therefore follow forth the course that I have begun, in planting colonies among them of answerable inlands subjects, that within short time may reform and civilise the best inclined among them, rooting out or transporting the barbarous and stubborn sort, and planting civilitie in their room.'

The MacGregors, whose chief held no superiority, had first become notorious in Queen Mary's reign, and now found how unfairly the 1587 Act pressed on a clan who lived on other men's lands. Landlords had no wish to make themselves responsible for the 'broken men' of other clans: so Menzies applied for a writ to eject MacGregor from lands in Rannoch, Sir Duncan Campbell of Glenorchy complained that the chief would not remove from Glenstrae and was acquitted of responsibility for him, and when MacGregor threw himself on the king's protection he was pardoned for past offences, but could neither find caution money nor control his clansmen. Losing patience, James resolved to make an example of 'the wicked and unhappie race of the clan Gregour', and gave orders 'to pursue and prosecute them with all rigour and extremetie'. A highly successful MacGregor raid culminated in the massacre of 200 Colquhouns in Glenfruin, only 12 miles from Dumbarton, in February 1603. A few months later, on the very day of King James's departure for London, his Privy Council passed an Act proscribing and abolishing the name, because 'the bair and simple name of McGregoure maid that haill Clane to presume of their power, force and strenthe, and did encourage them to go forward in thair iniquities'. The whole 'sickening story' of how the nameless clan were chased, starved, hanged, drowned, banished, branded and variously mauled and massacred out of existence is relieved only by the sympathy and pity aroused in their fellow Highlanders, who gave shelter to the victims even in distant parts like the Grant and Mackenzie countries.

Having shown James at his worst, it is only fair to recall that he also attempted more humane policies, especially from the broader base of the throne of Great Britain. Two commissioners, Andrew Stewart, Lord Ochiltree and Andrew Knox, Bishop of the Isles, were sent to treat with the island chiefs in 1608. After being summoned to a court held at Aros in Mull, they were shipped south and lodged in Dumbarton, Blackness and Stirling while

James made new plans for bringing peace and improved conditions to the Isles. He asked his Privy Council to consider future policy, not on the principle of exterminating or transplanting the inhabitants, but of devising means of introducing 'religion and civilitie' among them. The power and possessions of the chiefs were to be curtailed, their kinsmen who found fighting more profitable than farming were either to work or to leave the country, and the tillers of the soil were to enjoy the benefits of good government.

Bishop Knox was now sent to the Isles as the king's sole commissioner, all the imprisoned chiefs were set free, and in July 1609 nearly all the principal islanders met him in the Isle of Iona and gave their consent to nine 'statutes', which struck at some of the roots of clan power. They provided for the strengthening of the Reformed Church, the establishment of inns for the convenience of travellers, the control of import and production of wines and liquor, the suppression of idle vagabonds and beggars (including the bards) and the limitation of each chief's retinue, prohibition of carrying firearms, and sending the heirs of men of substance to the Lowlands for education. The chiefs became bound to observe these statutes, and to appear before the council at stated intervals: a new provision was later added that no one should inherit property in the Isles unless he could read, write and speak English – as we understand all the island chiefs could do now.

Meantime a different pattern was emerging in the north. The Mackenzies were becoming a separate power, comparable with the Gordons and the Campbells, their chief ennobled in 1609 and made Earl of Seaforth in 1623, and with the acquisition of Lewis from the 'Fife adventurers' his lands stretched from Cromarty to the Hebrides. In Badenoch, Strathspey, and the valleys of the Nairn and Findhorn, the confederacy of Clan Chattan was developing among those related by blood to the Mackintosh chiefs, and small independent clans seeking his protection. In 1609, arising out of 'controversies, quarrels, questions and hosts' within the clan, a great gathering of Macphersons, Macqueens, Macbeans and MacGillivrays, Shaws and Macleans of the north bound themselves and their successors to assist and defend Mackintosh as their chief, and to stand by each other on all occasions. By 1622 Mackintosh was being given royal authority to use the military services of the whole Clan Chattan, 'quhairever they dwell'.

A sign that the government was prepared to trust clans instead of always dictating policy to them was the calling of a three-day 'conference' at Edinburgh in 1624, when 36 Highland landlords met with 21 members of the Privy Council to discuss the preservation order and the treatment of the Clan Gregor remnant. The outcome was a plan for two Highland 'captaincies', one for Strathearn, Menteith and the Lennox, and the other for the Atholl region; two Stewarts were appointed 'His Majesty's Captains', with 20 men under each, to co-operate when necessary for policing the Highland region under their charge. This was a new departure, and similar policies were pursued after King James's death in 1625. Sporadic disturbances in the Highlands had not been eradicated, but it was to be religious and political differences on a national scale, and not purely local disputes, which led to the downfall of the Stewarts and, along with economic and social changes, to the collapse of the clan system.

Under Which King?

BELOW When the men of Mackay's Regiment arrived at Stettin in 1630 as part of the army of King Gustavus Adolphus of Sweden, an illustrated broadside showed the garments worn and the weapons carried by the strangers, and explained their ability to march long distances and subsist on little food

Highland soldiers fought in many of the armies of Europe, and earned fame for their endurance of hardship and their fiery impetuosity. In the seventeenth and eighteenth centuries they took a leading part in the religious, political and dynastic wars which convulsed their native land, and in the end the impact which shook a throne led to the eclipse of the clan system.

During this period the clans rose to national importance in British history and showed their merits and defects as fighting units. Their abilities put a powerful force at the disposal of their natural leaders, which in emergencies could be used to support or to disrupt the state.

Their tactics in battle were to charge up to the enemy's line, drop to the ground to avoid his fire and to discharge their own volley, and then to abandon their muskets and rush in with the sword. When on campaign, they lived on the country (if a Highland army could not plunder, it must be paid and fed); they might slip away on a private quarrel or to deposit their booty and provide for their families; and if the famous Highland charge once failed, they could seldom be rallied. But if this period saw the high water-mark of the national impact of the clans, in it were also sown the seeds of the breakdown of the clan system: this was not the outcome of

In folchem Habit Gehen die 800 In Stettin angekommen Irrländer oder Irren.

a single battle or even a campaign, but rather of a political, social and economic revolution which ran concurrently but not always steadily with the alternate tide of war and peace.

King James had tried to end the need to employ clansmen as soldiers at home, and his son Charles gave them official encouragement to serve under foreign flags. In the Swedish service one John Campbell was recommended in 1611 as being able to bring a knowledge of Gaelic to the task of drilling recruits, and under Gustavus Adolphus 'Mackay's Regiment' won lasting renown in the Thirty Years War. They were his 'right hand in battle, brought forward in all dangerous enterprises', and earned from their enemies the name of the 'Invincible old Regiment'.

The Mackay chief, Sir Donald of Farr (later Lord Reay), secured a licence from Charles I and his Privy Council to raise 3000 men for service in Germany in support of the king's sister Elizabeth and her husband the King of Bohemia, who was at war with Austria. As many as 1000 of Mackay's original contingent in 1626 were said to be his own 'immediate clansmen' from Sutherland; Robert Monro was chronicler of the regiment's deeds. The Highlands were a favourite recruiting ground: when Mackay came home to make up his numbers, King Charles asked Lord Lorne, Argyll's son, to use his influence in recruiting, as a 'readie supplie' of men could only be expected from 'the Northern parts and Ilands' of Scotland because of levies already made in the 'south and middle shires'.

It is tempting to assume that the kilt was the great distinguishing dress of Mackay's Regiment, or at least of its Highland companies, but there is no reference to their uniform in written sources. The only clue is to be found in a German print or broadside which depicts four *Irrländer* at Stettin (where Mackay's was quartered in 1630–31) – two of them with philabeg or belted plaid, one with a long coat open in front and legs bare, and one with jerkin, baggy knee-breeches and stockings, and all wearing striped bonnets. In each case the cloth resembles some sort of tartan, being 'woven in squares with bands and stripes' (as the folklorist J.F. Campbell put it); men drawn up in the background seem to wear belted plaids or kilts to the knee.

At home the great civil war had two 'curtain-raisers' in the Bishops' Wars of 1639 and 1640, when the king's attempt to increase the political power of the bishops was challenged in the National Covenant adopted by the Estates of Parliament in 1638. The two magnates with the widest Highland domains were Argyll,

who was head of the Covenanting party, and Huntly, the king's principal supporter in the North. Huntly's Gordons were at first held in check by a Covenant army under Montrose (in which some veterans of the Continental wars were serving); Argyll operated mainly in the west, but when he brought his Highlanders to the camp near Berwick 'these souple fellows, with their playds, targes, and dorlachs (dirks)' seemed strange in southern eyes.

A new covenant, the Solemn League and Covenant of 1643, aimed at securing ecclesiastical uniformity in Scotland and England, led to a renewal of the war. Montrose, a born leader of fighting men, and now the king's lieutenant-general, led a mixed force of Highlanders and Irish in a series of rapid marches and sudden attacks. Exiled MacDonalds and Macleans, brought back by Alasdair ('Colkitto') of the old Islay family, were joined by the clans of the middle Highlands – MacDonalds of Glengarry, Keppoch, Clanranald and Sleat, Macleans from Mull and Morvern, Stewarts from Appin, Farquharsons from Braemar, Camerons from Lochaber – united 'for the first time since Harlaw' not so much for king or covenant, but in hatred against the Campbells of Argyll. Montrose saw the fighting mettle of the clans, welded them into an army, and kept them

BELOW The leading presbyterian statesman Archibald Campbell, eighth earl and first marquess of Argyll, a poor soldier but a shrewd politician, painted in his late forties showing a powerful face, though worn and drawn

together in a campaign of a year's duration. He also knew their country, brought the Campbells' foes into the heart of Argyll's lands, and led them through snow-filled passes to surprise and rout his enemy at Inverlochy. Only when he returned to organised Lowland warfare was he defeated.

After the king's execution in 1649, Cromwell came north and defeated a Scottish army at Dunbar. A royalist detachment (mainly Highland) attempting to cross the Forth was cut to pieces at Inverkeithing, and the Highlanders suffered terribly in Cromwell's final victory at Worcester, after which several thousand were taken prisoner and shipped off to Barbados.

General George Monck, to whom Cromwell entrusted the subjection of Scotland, realised the importance of mastering the Highlands.

Forts were built at Inverness and Inverlochy, garrisons established in Dunnottar, Dunstaffnage, Dunollie, Duart, Blair Atholl and Dunkeld. Taking advantage of war with Holland, one more rising followed, with a force which rose to some 4000 under the Earl of Glencairn and then General Middleton. Ignoring Argyll's curse and the Campbell chieftains' warning, Lord Lorne joined the Royalists along with Glengarry, Seaforth and other chiefs. But Monck made a remarkable march lasting four weeks out from Perth which carried his cavalry, dragoons and foot soldiers through the wilds of Glengarry, Kintail and Strathfarrar where 'never any horse men (much less an armie)' had ever been seen before. Middleton was routed near Loch Garry and parts of the Highlands where insurgents might find shelter were devastated, but the chiefs were allowed to keep arms for their own and their tenants' defence. The Highlands were at peace under the usurper's heel.

When Charles II regained his throne at the Restoration in 1660, military rule ended, the forts and garrisons were 'slighted' and abandoned, and a new form of native 'police force' gradually began to emerge. Argyll was arraigned on a long list of charges and executed, although his Royalist son was soon back in favour; landlords and chiefs were summoned to renew their bonds for peace; some long-standing feuds were settled, but a new crop of 'fire and sword' commissions showed that the old disorders had not ended. In 1666 Charles authorized Argyll to form a 'watch' (for one year) of not more than 60 men to defend his own shire against robbers; a year later the Earl of Atholl was commissioned to raise men as a 'constant guard' for securing the peace of the Highlands, and to put down cattle thieves and 'blackmailers'; and this commission was continued to Sir James Campbell of Lawers and Major George Grant of the Freuchie family. Two new Highland companies, raised in 1678 under Lawers and Colonel James Menzies of Culdares had their first military service when Argyll waged war on the Macleans.

A sign that these companies were not quite equal to their task is that some 70 lairds, including several clan chiefs, were named in 1682 as commissioners to be responsible for the peace of their own districts; but in 1685 Captain Kenneth Mackenzie of Suddie (of the Earl of Mar's Regiment) received a special commission from James VII to arrest thieves and robbers and to recover stolen goods. Three years later, while helping the Mackintoshes to execute a Privy Council commission against

RIGHT The Stuart cause was not in the end triumphant, but it was to remain an active force in the Highlands for another 100 years. Charles II (centre) raised local companies to keep order, the birth of his nephew Prince James (left) precipitated the Revolution which forced the Stuarts from the throne and James's son Charles Edward (right) found his chief support among the Highland clans

the Macdonalds of Keppoch in Lochaber, Suddie fell at Mulroy in a sharp skirmish which turned out to be 'the last considerable clan-battle fought in the Highlands'.

But the clans were soon to be called to war on a wider issue. The birth of a son to the Catholic King James in June 1688 – just two months before Mulroy – precipitated the Revolution, which in turn brought about the re-establishment of the presbyterian form of church government in Scotland. William III of Orange (whose wife Mary was a Stewart princess) landed at Torbay, and received wide support, and James slipped away to France. In Scotland the Estates resolved that he had forfeited the crown, and William and Mary were proclaimed king and queen at Edinburgh. But episcopacy still retained a hold, particularly in the Gaelic Highlands: John Graham of Claverhouse (Viscount Dundee), who raised King James's standard, had few recruits until he secured help among the Highland clans. The 'fiery cross', a symbolic call to arms in the shape of two charred sticks fastened in the middle, went out through the glens, and Claverhouse met some of the chiefs in Lochaber in May 1689. An heroic poem in Latin, *The Grameid*, describes the scene in graphic detail as Camerons, MacDonalds and

Macleans, Macneils and many others gathered at Mucomir, where the Spean falls into the Lochy. Graham had won their confidence, and he made full use of the Highlanders' skill in moving quickly through their native hills and passes. The government's Gaelic-speaking commander, General Hugh Mackay (a Sutherland soldier raised in the Netherlands service) failed to win active support for Dutch William even among the Whig families in the North. Dundee seized Blair Castle, and when Mackay marched north to retake it they met in the narrow Pass of Killiecrankie (27 July) where the terrain suited the Highlanders, and a wild charge downhill broke Mackay's inexperienced troops, but in the rout Dundee was killed and the campaign eventually lost for King James.

More Highland companies were raised, garrisons established, and Fort William strengthened with stone ramparts. Those who took the oath acknowledging William and Mary by the end of 1691 were to be pardoned, and emissaries sent to James brought back word that his loyal subjects should do what might be best for their safety. Many chiefs postponed their transfer of allegiance to the last moment, and some of the most influential, including Cameron of Lochiel and MacDonell of Glengarry, had still not submitted when, in February 1692,

a bungled attempt to 'extirpate' the MacDonalds of Glencoe as a warning to others led to the massacre of nearly 40 people in the snow-filled glen by troops who had been quartered on them. William had signed the order personally, his Secretary of State was forced to resign, and many (but not yet all) hastened to submit.

After the Revolution the government dropped the practice of making clan chiefs stand surety for one another and their clans, and the Scots Privy Council to whom they had been answerable ceased to exist after the Union of the Parliaments in 1707. The clans were settling into an alignment of Jacobites against Whigs, their loyalties dictated mainly by religious, political or economic factors. A definite anti-Jacobite wedge had taken shape, separating the episcopalian Jacobites of Aberdeen and the north-east, from their Highland sympathizers in the Catholic and episcopalian coastal fringe and islands; the wedge consisted of the Campbells in the west, the families of Reay and Sutherland, Rosses and Munros in the north, and lesser houses like the Brodies and Roses, along with the bulk of the Grants and Forbeses of Culloden. This was significant in the campaigns which were to follow.

Profiting from the unpopularity of the Union, and seeking a 'second front' to relieve

RIGHT During the long exile of the Jacobites after the Revolution, Scottish officers became familiar figures on the Continent. This ivory snuff mull, probably carved in France, shows a Highland gentleman fully armed with broadsword, pistol, dirk and targe, and wearing a belted plaid and bonnet
BELOW *Glencoe*, by Horatio McCulloch. '. . . that pass is the most dreary and melancholy of all the Scottish passes, the very Valley of the Shadow of Death', wrote Macaulay in his *History*

the pressure on the French by Marlborough, Jacobite agents were busy preparing for a rising. A French fleet actually reached the Firth of Forth in 1708, and the dread remained of a landing in some remote part of the Highlands. One of the Privy Council's last acts before it expired was to call the chiefs of clans to Edinburgh, but nobody there had authority to examine them, and some suspected of Jacobite sympathies were carried off to London. The Duke of Gordon and his son Huntly, Seaforth, Sir Donald MacDonald, Lochiel and Stewart of Appin were in and out of custody in the south for some weeks after the invasion fleet had returned to base.

Some attempt was made to reorganise and extend the Highland Companies, now becoming known as the Independent Companies, as they formed distinct units unconnected with each other. Their 'peculiar clothing' of 'plads, tartan coats, trousers and hose', was, according to a War Office report in 1709, 'not at all military, but like the clothing of the natives there, that they may the better discover any designs or machinations against the Government or the country'. This clothing was provided by their officers, and was not yet of a uniform pattern, but it was apparently their 'sombre appearance' which had earned for them

the title *Am Freiceadan Dubh* ('Black Watch') to distinguish them from the *Cotaichean* or *Saighdearan Dearg* (redcoats) who formed the permanent garrison at Inverlochy.

The next alarm came with the illness of Queen Anne, whose Tory ministry were not unfavourable to the 'Chevalier' (as Prince James was called) as her successor. But when the Queen died in 1714, the Whigs saw to it that the Elector of Hanover (a great-grandson of James VI, his mother being a daughter of Elizabeth of Bohemia) should come over to reign as George I. The Earl of Mar, out of office as Secretary of State, summoned the Scottish Jacobites to meet him, and raised the standard for King James on the Braes of Mar. MacDonalds, Camerons, Mackenzies, Mackintoshes, Macphersons, Macleans and others joined Mar in the brief campaign of 1715. His strength was reckoned at 11,140, plus 3000 from Atholl and Breadalbane who went into rebellion without their superiors; clans well-affected to King George totalled about 8000 men, of which half were Argyll's. 300 Frasers who were on the march with Mar were withdrawn on the sudden return of Simon (heir-male of Lovat) from an enforced exile to assume the chiefship. Some of the more northern Jacobites were delayed in Easter Ross

Between the two Jacobite Risings, General George Wade was tireless in his endeavours to disarm the Highlanders and to open up the country. His portrait by J. B. Van Loo as a field marshal ABOVE shows the famous bridge over the Tay at Aberfeldy, constructed by him in 1732–34 to designs by William Adam, which remains today as his finest monument ABOVE, RIGHT OPPOSITE A map by C. Lempriere, dated 1731, includes the lines of 'new road' built through the Highlands, plans of the three forts in the Great Glen, and the strength and distribution of the clans

44

LEFT John Campbell, 4th earl of Loudoun, who later commanded in North America, was painted by Allan Ramsay 'in the regimentals of his Highland Regiment' (raised 1745, disbanded 1748) ABOVE Ruthven barracks in Badenoch, on a mound above the Spey opposite Kingussie, were built in 1719

BELOW A skirmish in Glenshiel in the same year, when there was a Jacobite invasion attempt with Spanish aid, inspired a modern painting by Lionel Edwards showing the grey horses of Campbell's Dragoons and mortars in action
A private soldier of the 42nd Regiment of Foot OPPOSITE, BELOW appears

in an official 'clothing book' of the British regular forces in 1742 – the earliest known illustration showing Highland dress worn as military uniform. In one of many sketches from Continental sources about this time OPPOSITE, ABOVE the belted plaid hangs down from the waist in two figures and over the shoulders in a third

through opposition by the Whig clans. Argyll had taken the field for the government, and after a confused fight at Sheriffmuir, Mar withdrew to Perth; a Jacobite force which had entered England was defeated at Preston on the same day. James arrived in time to wind up the rising, and left after less than two months in Scotland.

Once military action ceased, a rather half-hearted effort was made to prevent a repetition. Scottish sentiment was outraged by the removal of some prisoners for trial in England, but less than 30 were hanged, and some of the ring-leaders escaped from prison. Mar, Tullibardine, Seaforth and about ten other Highland chiefs were attainted and their estates forfeited to the crown, and the carrying of arms was forbidden north of the Forth. But Jacobite feeling was so prevalent, and so many Scots had relatives involved in the rising, that on various pretexts some of the forfeitures were ineffective, and serviceable arms were retained while useless ones were given up.

Foreign backing led to another brief 'attempt' in 1719, though a concurrent invasion of England failed to materialize. A Spanish contingent was landed in Kintail, Eilean Donan was garrisoned, and Tullibardine, Seaforth, Lochiel and Lord George Murray with men from Atholl made up an expeditionary force. Regular troops with militia from Ross and Sutherland were sent out from Inverness, and they defeated and dispersed the invaders in a skirmish in Glenshiel.

A more serious attempt to settle the problem of law and order in the Highlands was made under General George Wade, who came to Scotland as Commander of the Forces in 1725 and remained until 1740. As shown in a map by Lempriere he had a network of nearly 250 miles of metalled roads and innumerable bridges constructed to serve the Great Glen forts, the barracks in Glenelg and Ruthven in Badenoch, and to link Inverness with Crieff and Dunkeld, crossing the mountains at the passes of Drumochter and Corrieyarick. He revived the Independent Companies (disbanded in 1717), and had about 500 men raised in 1725 by six commanders well disposed to the government (three Campbells, and one each from the Grants, Frasers and Munros). Like their predecessors, they wore Highland dress, but Wade introduced a measure of uniformity by ordering that each company's plaids were to be 'as near as they can of the same sort and colour'. In 1739, while Great Britain was at war with Spain, the six Independent Companies were increased to ten, and formed into a regular Regiment 780 strong – later

RIGHT A vivid impression of what men of the Highland Regiment looked like while on the march in Flanders is given in this contemporary series of engravings. A mounted captain, a lieutenant (followed by his wife) and an ensign (carrying the regimental colour) appear in the upper three panels. Clothing, weapons and musical instruments are clearly shown (but no pipers), and also a vehicle for the sick and wounded, and a baggage horse. The series, captioned in French and German, is dated at Mainz on the Rhine in 1743 (bottom left); the colouring, added by a later hand, should not be taken seriously

em Gewehr.
ur l'epaule.

Bewaffnete Schotten mit Schildt u. Schwerdt.
Ecossois armé d'un bouclier avec un sabre.

Bergschotten mit übergeschlagener Decke.
Ecossois montagns ard avec ine colverture.

weichen keinen.
ges uns hilfft.

Der Schild der deckt den Leib, das Schwerd
Wir rufen aber nicht, biß wir gerochen
das dreht den Feind.
seynd.

Ihr Schild und Schwerdt verlasst so schau,
Und greif alsdann geschwind nach Messer
und Pistol.

Das Feur Rohr pflegen wir geschickt und
wohl zu führen,
Durch dessen Kraft soll der Feind das Leben
auch verliehren.

Wagen-Meister.
Maistre des chariots.

Marode und Krancke.
Adro de et Malades.

Wagen-Knecht.
Valets des chariots.

nehmen nur
in meiner

Marod, Bagag, Gewehr die pfleg ich nach,
Damit sich auf dem Weg keins dessen
mag verzehren.

Ich bin malad und schwach, u. kan nicht
mehr fort,
Daß nichts zurücke bleib, drum pflegt
man uns zu führen.

Ich Franck u. Frau, ist gleich mein Kind
führt mir die Speiß
Dieweil wir nicht ergehen die Speiß in
diesem Land.

Ich aber mach dem Marsch ein End, und
Und faß den Wagen an, daß solcher nicht
kan wancken.

Schotten die das Gewehr vor dem Regen bedecken.
Ecossois couvre les armes contre la pluie.

Feld Music.
Musique Champetre.

Schotten mit Feur Rohr, Pi
Ecossois avec fusil, pist

stohl, Schwerd, Bajo
et, Sabre, Bajon

net u. Messer
et couau.

Sind uns will im
reff nach Schotten

Durch meine Feld Schalmey ermuntre ich
Der Schotten offtermahls zum Spielen Tanzen Springen.

Die Tromel rühre ich, mein Stück wie
Drum läßt der Schotte auch auf seinen
auch hüpft tanzen.

Feur Rohr, Pallasch, Pistohl, Messer und Ba-
Das führt ein Schott zu Feld, damit sein
Feind zu kehren.

Schottische Ba gagage.
Bagage d'Ecossois.

Feld Zimmerleuth.
Charpentieres.

Pfeiffer.
Riffleurs.

Tambour.
Tambours.

Feld Scherer.
Chyrurgiens.

Servis, Bagag
gue Ariegen

Wir aber seyn bestellt zu Steeg und Brug.
Und wanns die Noth geheißt die Wälder zu
verhauen.

Durch unser Music wird der Berg Schott
Und geht Kecker zu Feld zu suchen eine
Beut.

Der muntre Tromel Schlag erfreut auch
Und frischt zum Schlagen an die tapfere
Hochlander.

Wird einer dann blessirt an Kopf, Leib
So thu mit Pflaster ich den solchen gleich
verbinden.

The two romantic figures of the Forty-Five – Prince Charles Edward Stuart, from Antonio David's portraits LEFT and Flora MacDonald, painted by Richard Wilson RIGHT: the handsome young leader of the attempt to win back the throne for his family, and one of the many who helped him to evade capture during his wanderings after Culloden. A reward of £30,000 was offered, and a 'likeness notwithstanding the disguise' circulated OPPOSITE, but although many knew his hiding-places none came forward to claim it

LEFT A coloured print of a Highland soldier, here seen with his wife and child wrapped in a shawl of the same tartan, by Martin Englebrecht

famous as the 42nd Highlanders, Royal Highland Regiment, or Black Watch. The men wore a kilt of dark green 'Government' tartan, belted plaid, and blue bonnet with black cockade. This dress was approved by King George, before whom a sergeant and private soldier 'performed their exercises' in January 1740, in presence of the Duke of Cumberland and general officers. The regiment, after an initial setback which led to mutiny, were sent to Flanders, where they covered themselves with glory when allowed 'their own way of fighting' at Fontenoy, and earned high praise for their behaviour to the civil population. Another regiment, under John Earl of Loudoun, was in process of being raised in the Highlands in 1745 when Prince Charles Edward Stewart arrived in Scotland with seven companions to claim the throne of his ancestors.

After a brief landing at Eriskay in the Outer Hebrides, the prince reached Loch nan Uamh and set foot on the Scottish mainland on 25 July. He raised his father's standard at Glenfinnan on 19 August, when the neighbouring clans began to gather after some initial reluctance by the chiefs who had expected him to bring an army. His main support came from the West Highlands, Camerons, MacDonalds and

Manifesto X

Cooper de fe Edinburgh 1745.

A likeness notwithstanding the Disguise that any Person who Secures the Son of the
Pretender is Intitled to a Reward of 30.000 £.

the government commander had been beaten at Prestonpans, and for a month Charles held court at Holyroodhouse. Then came the disastrous march to Derby, the failure of the English Jacobites to rise, and the retreat back to Scotland, a brief success at Falkirk, and the long trail north. But the government had taken fright, and the king's second son, William Duke of Cumberland, was sent to Scotland, marched round the coast by Aberdeen, and practised his regular troops in how to resist the Highland charge. Crossing the Spey, he met the Jacobite army drawn up on ill-chosen ground on Drumossie Moor near Culloden on 16 April, when the clans who had followed Prince Charles fought under their chiefs and suffered defeat in the final battle of the campaign. The duke's next three months in Scotland fixed on him the name of 'Butcher', while his cousin, whose army was dispersed, took to the heather and became the hunted 'Bonnie Prince Charlie' of legend as for five months he evaded capture, with a price of £30,000 on his head which the loyalty of the clans who gave him shelter scorned to win by betraying him.

It was as military units that the clans made this last appearance on the national stage, and it is for their bravery and loyalty in a 'lost cause' that they are chiefly remembered today. The clan regiments, large and small, were not of course composed of men all bearing the same surname, any more than were the clans themselves. Chiefs and their families and cadets naturally supplied an important part of the commissioned officers; some units were stronger than others in men of one surname; and the Mackintosh regiment, for instance, included men of all the Clan Chattan names, and was commanded by MacGillivray of Dunmaglass, while in another case many Robertsons from the Struan estate served in the Atholl Brigade. After the rising was crushed, frequent pleas were put forward by Jacobite prisoners that they had been forced out; and it has been fairly argued that some of those serving with government units were as much 'forced men' as some who served the prince. Nor were bravery or suffering a monopoly of either side, and in one clan with a consistently anti-Jacobite record the chief and his two brothers fell in the king's service. Although the clans on both sides wore tartan, it was not so much by this as by the colour of the badge or cockade in their bonnets – black for King George, white for King James – that they were distinguished.

If so many clans had not risen in the 'Fifteen' and 'Forty-Five', it is unlikely that the settled

ABOVE A drawing of Charles Edward soon after landing in Moidart taking leave of Antoine Walsh who provided and commanded the frigate which carried him from France was presented to Walsh by the Prince soon after his return
In Scotland today many old memories linger; at Glenfinnan the statue of a kilted Highlander surmounts a monument at the head of Loch Shiel OPPOSITE ABOVE, and at Culloden the clan graves are still carefully tended OPPOSITE BELOW

Stewarts from Lochaber, Glengarry, Moidart and Appin; from the north-east lowlands of Moray, Banff and Aberdeen; and from Badenoch and Perthshire. The north was mainly for the government, and most (but not all) of the Mackenzies, ruined by previous devotion to the cause, did not rise for the prince; the MacDonalds of Sleat and the MacLeods of Dunvegan were held back by the influence of Lord President Forbes of Culloden; and the Frasers waited to see which side their chief would choose to support. Jacobite estimates of strength vary from above 8000 to 10,000 men, while irregular forces and volunteers on the government side have been calculated at over 12,000, joined ultimately by three Scottish regiments.

Within two months of the prince's first landing, however, Edinburgh had surrendered,

government and the Hanoverian succession would have been put in danger. They paid the price of the fear they had inspired, and the resolve that there must be no repetition. As one sure remedy, Cumberland even advised the transportation of whole clans such as the Camerons and MacDonalds to the West Indies. Lord Chancellor Hardwicke suggested proscribing the names of some of the clans, as had been done by James VI to the MacGregors. But in fact other counsels prevailed, and other ways were found, to ensure that the clans as military units should never again be a menace to the peace of the state.

PAGES 54–55 A contemporary picture (based on a drawing by A. Heckel) shows how the battle developed, with the Jacobites attempting to break the line of Government troops with a Highland charge, the others' reliance on discipline and controlled fire power, and the outflanking and destruction of the Jacobite army by cavalry and sheer numbers

The BATTLE of

This View of the Glorious Victory obtained over the Rebels shews His MAJESTIES Army commanded by His Royal Hig[...]
[...]ody of Reserve, composed of Four ‑ Part of the Highland Army is here represented as furiously attempting with Swor[...]
[...]nets of Barrels & Munro's intrepid Regiments. The right wing of the Rebels being cover'd by a stone Wall, Kerr & Co[...]
[...]put them into immediate confusion. Kingstons Horse wheel'd off at the same time by the right of ij Kings, for[...]

LODEN April 16. 1746.

Duke of *CUMBERLAND*, drawn up in three Lines; the Front consisting of Six Battallions of Foot, the Second of Five, the Third was

ts to break in upon the left of the Dukes front Line, where their Rashnefs met with it's deserved chastisement from the Fire and

agoons under *Hawley & Bland*, are describ'd as passing through a breach that had been made for them in it, to attack the rear of

g on the left of the Rebels met our Dragoons in their Center, on which began the total rour of these disturbers of the *Publick Repose*

Dispersal

RIGHT Of the three Great Glen forts, only Fort William had held out against the Jacobites. A new Fort George was built to replace Wade's fort at Inverness, and Fort Augustus, which had fallen after a two-day siege, had to be repaired – this water-colour by Sandby shows the bastions 'slighted' and the buildings roofless

A serious attempt to break up the clans for ever was made after the battle of Culloden. Cumberland moved his troops from Inverness to Fort Augustus, from where parties were sent out through the glens to hunt down known Jacobites, burn houses and carry off cattle, while others operated in the Isles, the north-west, and in Badenoch. When Lord President Forbes spoke to Cumberland of this process of pacification, and mentioned the laws of the country, the duke is said to have replied, 'I'll make a brigade give laws.'

But Parliament, though it voted an extra £25,000 a year for 'signal services' in suppressing the 'wicked and unnatural rebellion', showed a different attitude in a series of 'clan acts' largely promoted by the Lord Chancellor, Hardwicke. An Act of Attainder, 1746, listed 41 persons as traitors, and more than 80 were actually excepted from the general pardon; an Act for disarming the Highlands and 'restraining' (or rather proscribing) the use of Highland dress followed; a Vesting Act forfeited the estates of all attainted persons to the crown; and the Heritable Jurisdictions Act abolished most of the rights on which the chiefs' power over their clansmen was supposed to rest.

The administration of the forfeited estates, and particularly of the 14 'inalienably' annexed to the crown by a further Act in 1752, was of enduring benefit. Old forms of agriculture and tenancy were changed, new types of work introduced, and social and economic conditions improved throughout the mainly Jacobite areas. Sheriffs appointed by the crown became responsible for law and order, and great feudal nobles like Argyll, Huntly and Atholl lost much of their power, over £150,000 being paid in compensation which could be used to improve their estates. Their authority as chiefs was of course mainly patriarchal, but in the end this too wilted before the advance of a 'money economy'.

On the military side, the mapping of even the most inaccessible places in the Highlands under Generals Watson and Roy was part of the post-'45 occupation, and so was the building of a new and stronger Fort George on a barren peninsula projecting into the Moray Firth some nine miles east of Inverness. Quite the most arbitrary measure was the 'clothing' section of the Disarming Act, which forbade the wearing of the Highland garb or any part of it from August 1747. The time for the compulsory change was twice extended, but in December 1748 the army was ordered to enforce it strictly, seizing all offenders and hailing them 'in the same dress' before a civil magistrate to convince him of their guilt. Penalty for a first offence was six months' imprisonment, and for a second transportation for seven years; later, an offender might be legally enlisted, if fit to be a soldier, on the instructions of a justice or judge.

None could quarrel with the right of any government to take away the weapon that is lifted against it (although it was hard that the clans who had defended the king should now be forbidden to defend themselves, as Dr Johnson put it), but the proscription of the Highland dress caused great sorrow and indignation, and

In the Roy survey all parts of Scotland were mapped in sufficient detail for future planning. Sections shown illustrate OPPOSITE, ABOVE land on the shores of the Cromarty Firth and ABOVE the area in Badenoch where the Wade road from Perth to Inverness divided before reaching the Spey, the western branch going up-river to the Corrieyarick Pass, while the main route made for Ruthven barracks. Surveying parties like the one seen in Rannoch OPPOSITE, BELOW were kept busy for several years in the field before the work was complete

has been widely condemned. Johnson called it 'an ignorant wantonness of power', and Scott 'a very harsh regulation'; but the latter admitted that 'there was a knowledge of mankind in the prohibition, since it divested the Highlanders of a dress which was closely associated with their habits of clanship and of war'. Tartan had indeed become a Jacobite symbol, for in Edinburgh, eight months after Culloden, it was rumoured that the Prince's birthday was to be celebrated by dinners and balls at which ladies would wear 'tartan gowns with shoes and stockings of the same kind' and white ribbons.

Duncan Forbes thought it 'an utter impossibility, without the advantage of this dress, for the inhabitants to tend their cattle, and to go through the other parts of their business, without which they could not subsist, not to speak of paying rents to their landlords'. Gaelic bards might praise the 'flowing tartan' and anathematize 'the breeks' (as the hated Lowland trousers were called), and reluctant clansmen carry them on a stick over their shoulders, but the law took its course. Many were sent to prison, the most absurd case being that of Oronoco, a black servant whom Stewart of Appin had rigged out in tartan livery, who was arrested in Rannoch and committed to

prison. Finally, a youth was seized for wearing a kilt which it turned out was stitched up the middle so as to have 'something of the form of the trousers worn by Dutch skippers', and handed over to a recruiting officer by the sheriff who convicted him. His friends protested, and the case was carried to the Court of Session where an acquittal led to such evasions of the Act being more leniently treated. Renewed by Parliament for seven years a few months before George II's death in 1760, it seems to have fallen into desuetude, though not actually repealed for another 20 years.

Transportation as a punishment formed an important factor in the dispersal of the clans. About 120 men actually taken in rebellion were executed, 936 were ordered to be transported to the plantations in the West Indies and America, and a further 222 banished or forbidden to return to the country (a 'genteel' form of transportation). This was no new thing – there had been Highlanders among the royalist prisoners sent to Boston after the battle of Worcester, and some 600 Jacobites had been shipped in 1716 as indentured servants to Antigua, South Carolina, Maryland and Virginia.

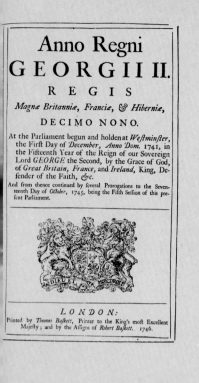

ABOVE The 'Clothing Act', officially known as 19 Geo. II cap. 39, was primarily an Act for disarming the Highlanders, but stiff penalties were imposed for wearing any part of the Highland dress

A few voluntary emigrations from the Highlands are on record before 1745. Sir Aeneas Macpherson of Invereshie had a grant of 5000 acres in Pennsylvania (1685); many Highland gentlemen and 'planters' went to the Scottish colony of Darien in 1698/9; Sir Ewen Cameron of Lochiel acquired land in the West Indies, and in 1734 a grandson took 'a cargo of people' from Lochaber to Jamaica. General Oglethorpe recruited some 130 colonists from Inverness-shire to defend the southern frontier of Georgia and, in compliment to the settlers, whom he found in 1736 wearing tartan plaids, and armed with broadswords, targes and muskets, he dressed himself in Highland costume and slept in the open wrapped in his cloak. Captain Lachlan Campbell, an Islay tacksman, who went to New York in 1737, arranged for about 500 emigrants, many of them from the Hebrides, to go out to the colony over the next three years; and in North Carolina 350 people from Argyll led by Duncan Campbell of Kilduskland settled in 1739 on the Upper Cape Fear River.

An indirect stimulus to further emigration came from the service of Highland regiments in America during the Seven Years War (1756–63). Hardwicke, who strongly disapproved of employing Highland soldiers and thought it a special 'act of imprudence' to give a former rebel the command of a battalion, resigned the Great Seal at the end of 1756. Argyll saw it as an indirect means of destroying 'disaffection', and the elder Pitt (later Earl of Chatham) persuaded George II to allow Highlanders to enter the military service of the crown. Two outstanding men were now commissioned to raise regiments in the Highlands – Archibald Montgomerie, a cheerful, high-spirited young man, son of the Earl of Eglinton, who though a Lowlander was able to recruit successfully in the north and south Highlands owing to his own character and his family connections, and Simon Fraser, the former Master of Lovat, attainted for his part in the '45 but later pardoned, and now able to raise 800 men on the forfeited Lovat estate alone through a family interest which transcended the feudal tie.

RIGHT Archibald Montgomerie, later eleventh earl of Eglinton, who was brother-in-law of Sir Alexander MacDonald of Sleat in Skye and Moray of Abercairney in Perthshire, raised the 78th Highlanders and led them in America under General Amherst. Sir Joshua Reynolds painted him wearing a diced and feathered bonnet and a plaid on his shoulders

FAR RIGHT An extract from Pitt's speech in the House of Commons, 14th January 1766
BELOW A weaver is seen at his loom in this picture of the inside of a cottage in Islay, from a drawing supplied by Sir Joseph Banks to the traveller Thomas Pennant

I have no local attachments: it is indifferent to me, whether a man was rocked in his cradle on this side or that side of the Tweed. I sought for merit wherever it was to be found. It is my boast, that I was the first minister who looked for it, and I found it in the mountains of the north. I called it forth, and drew it into your service, an hardy and intrepid race of men! men, who, when left by your jealousy, became a prey to the artifices of your enemies, and had gone nigh to have overturned the state, in the war before the last. These men, in the last war, were brought to combat on your side: they served with fidelity, as they fought with valour, and conquered for you in every part of the world: detested be the national reflections against them! they are unjust, groundless, illiberal, unmanly.

William Pitt (1766).

It was a bold experiment. A number of the officers had been 'out' for the prince a dozen years earlier, or were sons of fathers who had been, but even though they might be regarded as soldiers of fortune whose attachment to the House of Hanover was 'very small', the government had no cause to regret their confidence. Both units were 1460 strong, and there was a surplus for other regiments; they wore Highland dress, and as Montgomerie's Highlanders and Fraser's Highlanders (numbered the 77th and 78th Regiments of Foot) they helped to conquer Canada. Wolfe paid them this tribute: 'The Highlanders are very useful, serviceable soldiers, and commanded by the most manly corps of officers I have ever seen' (less humanely, in a private letter, he said: 'They are hardy, intrepid, accustomed to a rough country, and no great mischief if they fall. How can you better employ a secret enemy than by making his end conducive to the common good?') Several of the officers had been in the Scots units of the Dutch service, for which there was always a ready supply of young Highland recruits before a greater war intervened. Two further Highland regiments were raised for service in Europe, and many other Highlanders joined other units such as the 89th Regiment which helped to open up Bengal to British influence – and incidentally to many enterprising Scots for whom a passage to India was the first step on the road to wealth and influence. These were the men who, along with their comrades of the Black Watch, carried the fame of bonnet, plaid and bagpipes throughout the world, and whose soldierly qualities earned the praise given them by Chatham in a much-quoted passage of an otherwise unimportant speech.

ABOVE John Murray, fourth earl of Dunmore, was painted in 1765 by Reynolds in a red and black tartan jacket and 'Government' tartan kilt and plaid. He had been a page to Prince Charles Edward and was to be the unpopular Governor of Virginia

LEFT Thomas Faed's painting 'Oh, why left I my hame?' has in it the pathos of emigration from the highlands, as has Jacob Thompson's 'Highland Bride's Departure' RIGHT even if the farewell in this case is for a shorter journey

RIGHT The arrival of the ship *Hector* at Pictou, Nova Scotia, in September 1773, with about 200 emigrants who had sailed from Lochbroom in Wester Ross, is looked back to as the first wave of a mighty tide which has swept westwards across the Atlantic from the Scottish Highlands

LEFT Some of the families evicted from Glencalvie in Easter Ross found temporary shelter at Croick in Strathcarron, where they scratched messages on the windows of the Parliamentary church. One of these reads: 'Glencalvie people was in the churchyard, May 24 1845'

ABOVE All over the Highlands, particularly in the north and west and in the islands, the sites of vanished townships are marked among the bracken by rectangles of stones, all that is left of the walls of what once were homes. Calgary in the Isle of Mull is one such site – its name given by a friend of the owner to a new settlement in Canada which is now a great city

It was estimated that up to 12,000 Highlanders were enlisted in the Seven Years War, – although the figure has been put much higher. Casualties were severe – 'Were not Highlanders put upon every hazardous enterprise where nothing was to be got but broken bones?' Of one regiment originally 1200 strong only 76 men were said to have returned to Scotland, but that was largely because officers and men were offered grants of land according to their rank in Prince Edward Island and the Hudson valley. There they helped to expand the frontier of settlement, and provided a reservoir of trained soldiers who remained loyal to their country of origin. By letters and even visits home, they persuaded relatives and friends to join them, so that the 'clannish instinct' helped to promote further emigration and even directed it to particular places.

Despite the drain of men to the army, the population was in a few years greater than ever, and there were many without work. Even in the Highlands, a cash economy was gradually replacing the old pastoral way of life, and a wish for paid employment was spreading. The tacksmen, who used to call out and officer the clan in times of danger still had a role in the administration of large estates, but now that military service formed no part of the rent he paid to his landlord and chief he was often required to pay more in cash. A few who objected to higher rents might revenge themselves by persuading tenants to emigrate with them ('we shall carry a clan to America, and when they are there, they must work for us, or starve'), while those who wished to remain might want to get rid of lower tenants who were a liability in hard times. Some Highland landlords did lower their rents, in the hope of stemming emigration; those who would not allow the continuing subdivision of holdings were charged with tyranny and compelling younger sons to leave, while those who allowed it were blamed for the wretched condition of their estates and tenants.

During the dozen or so years between the peace of 1763 and the year when war broke out again in America, emigration from the Highlands reached what Dr Johnson called an 'epidemical fury'. Social readjustment, poverty, overpopulation, rising rents, bad seasons, and more shipping all contributed, but eviction (to make way for sheep or otherwise) did not come until later. The desire to safeguard savings and property, and an ambition for betterment, also played a part, but there is not much evidence of a wish to establish 'new clans in the other hemisphere' (of which Johnson also thought he saw signs) being in any way a particularly important factor.

Cattle raising was the main occupation of Highland farmers, but in the 1760s sheep farming was introduced from the Lowlands, and it spread rapidly as the century advanced. One of the first recorded evictions to enable land to be turned into a sheep-walk was beside Loch Laggan in Badenoch, where 80 people were forced out of their holdings at Aberarder on the forfeited Cluny estate under a judicial decree of 1770 but eviction was not given as a general reason for emigration until the 1790s.

Emigration could be spontaneous, and the causes and advantages of it were widely

discussed in pamphlets and periodicals. A group of 2000 from Skye planned to go as a 'formed colony' to one of the overseas settlements in 1771, organised themselves as a unit with minister and surgeon, and made the necessary arrangements themselves. Farther north, after a difficult winter, some tenants in Assynt were talking of emigration 'in imitation of the Skye scheme'.

By 1773, as well as plaintive songs inspired by emigration, Johnson and Boswell saw a lively dance in Skye which demonstrated how 'emigration catches till all are set afloat'. Of course those who left home suffered many

ABOVE Highlanders found their way to all parts of the world. The mighty Fraser River in Canada is named in honour of Simon Fraser, son of a British army officer serving in America, who followed its turbulent course from the Rocky Mountains to the sea

65

hardships, but as the pace grew faster the partings at least became less grievous; as Highlanders watched more of their kin depart for America, attachment to home and clan now worked in the cause of emigration. Something like 20,000 people are reckoned to have left the Highlands in the dozen years up to the War of Independence but there was an official ban on emigration to America from 1775 to 1783.

In the American struggle for independence there were Scots on both sides, but most of the first-generation immigrants remained loyal to the British crown. Some people have been puzzled why so many Highlanders should have aligned themselves with a Hanoverian monarch only a generation after 1745, but apart from the contemporary issues it has to be remembered that many of the clans had supported the government against the Jacobites, or at least remained neutral. Many Americans of Highland descent had no hesitation in supporting the 'patriot' side, including a MacDougall and a Mackintosh who rose to high rank and earned the praise of George Washington.

An old officer of Fraser's, Colonel Allan Maclean from Torloisk in Mull, raised a Royal Highland Emigrant Regiment, which gathered in many discharged soldiers of the 42nd, Fraser's and Montgomerie's Highlanders who had settled in Canada, while another battalion was raised under Major John Small from Strathardle in Perthshire. The Emigrants, numbered the 84th Regiment in 1778, wore full Highland dress (with sporrans of racoons' instead of badger skins), saw active service throughout the war, including a notable defence of Quebec, and they were rewarded with free grants of land in Canada.

Loyalists from the south settled in large numbers in Nova Scotia, New Brunswick and Ontario. After overcoming the initial difficulties, they encouraged others at home to follow, and in places such as Glengarry county at the eastern tip of Ontario, Highlanders continued to settle for many years. Emigration and trade were resumed after 1783, but the ties between Scotland and America had been loosened, and the focus of Scots immigration shifted north. The Scottish Highlands became a prolific nursery for the Canadian fur trade, the names of Mackenzie and Fraser pioneers were given to great rivers in the North-West, and McTavish and McGillivray tapped the vast resources of half a continent.

A REAL "SCOTTISH GRIEVANCE."

DUNCAN.—"Oh! but my mother is frail, and can't be sent out of the country in that ship; will you not let Flora and her ———"
FACTOR.—[sternly] "No, no lad—move on with the old woman, she will not be here in the way of his Lordship's sheep and deer."

London, Pub.

SPORTING MEETI

McLean, Jan.ʳ 1. 1820.

I. Clark sculp.ᵗ

in the HIGHLANDS.

The 'great dispersal' had been substantially begun, and as the years passed the flow increased in volume. One of the newer destinations was Australia, where a 'trickle' from Scotland (due partly to Governor Lachlan Macquarie's range of kin and friends in the west Highlands) became a stronger stream in the 1830s; at least one ship-load from the Hebrides wished to settle as a group, and many brought useful experience of sheep farming to the new continent.

Meantime at home, new economic pressures were leading to the 'clearances', and between the first and probably most trying eviction

RIGHT The great reputation as fighters earned by Highland regiments is shown by a Highland Society of London medal for the 42nd Highlanders designed by Benjamin West after Abercrombie's victory at Alexandria in 1801, and a Dundee token coin of 1797 inscribed 'From the Heath Covered Mountains of Scotia we Come'

The Highland soldiers' gallantry in the Crimea, at the battle of the Alma and in Balaclava's 'Thin Red Line', was celebrated in a painting by Felix Philippoteaux BELOW and a music sheet cover drawing of the 93rd (Sutherland) Highlanders engaging the Russian cavalry OPPOSITE, FAR RIGHT

period (up to 1820) and the second (after 1840) estates were changing hands at a rapid rate. Clanranald's bankruptcy threw Arisaig, Moidart and the Small Isles on the market; the Reay country was sold to the Duke of Sutherland, and soon afterwards Harris went to Lord Dunmore; the Duke of Gordon's lands in Badenoch and Lochaber passed into various hands, and South Uist and Benbecula went to Colonel Gordon of Cluny; Glengarry was bought by Lord Ward and Glenquoich by Edward Ellice; General Macneil sold Barra, and Inverlochy passed to Lord Abinger; but some of the old Highland families were returning with new-found wealth, like the Mathesons who bought back lands round Lochalsh, as well as Lewis and many other estates. Highland sport was becoming increasingly fashionable, but capital was also being spent on developing local resources.

After the long peace which followed Waterloo, the fame of the Highlands and the glamour of the tartan were again being carried to the outside world by the regiments which fought in the Crimea and in India. Highland dash was the deciding factor in the battle of the Alma (1854), when three battalions in Sir Colin Campbell's brigade stormed the heights above the river in face of twelve enemy battalions; and the classic example of steadiness in action was given when the 93rd Highlanders repelled a Russian cavalry charge at Balaklava. Seven Highland regiments served in the Indian Mutiny, when Sir Colin could again 'bring on the tartan' with a Highland brigade under his command, the 'pipes of Lucknow' inspired Whittier's verse, and before Cawnpore the 78th earned Havelock's tribute, 'I am not a Highlander, but I wish I was one.' With the founding of the Black Watch of Canada in 1862 (the oldest Highland regiment in any Dominion) a movement began which was to embrace many of Scottish descent overseas, and have important consequences in the two world wars of the twentieth century.

BELOW In the two world wars of the twentieth century, regiments from Canada and other parts of the Commonwealth brought many men of Highland descent to the aid of Great Britain and her allies
A water-colour by 'Snaffles' LEFT shows the kilt being worn in the trenches of World War I and Scott Sutherland's statue RIGHT of a soldier of World War II in battle-dress blouse and kilt is a feature of a Black Watch memorial near Dundee

Revival

The process by which the Scottish Highlands, with their clans and tartans, emerged from the gloomy aftermath of the 'Forty-Five' into the bright glare of pride and popularity is a curious blend of romantic, literary, military, political and industrial enterprise and enthusiasm.

A point of origin might be found in the publication in 1760 of a slim volume, entitled *Fragments of Ancient Poetry collected in the Highlands of Scotland and translated from the Galic or Erse Language,* followed by English versions of two 'ancient epic poems' attributed to Ossian, son of a Gaelic prince of the third

century. A collection of the *Works of Ossian* (1765) produced a tremendous literary explosion, in which national pride and prejudice were involved on an unbelievable scale, and whose echoes are still occasionally heard. The author-translator was James Macpherson, a Badenoch schoolmaster, and the genuineness of his 'originals' became controversial enough to send two generations of literary inquirers scouring the Highlands and Hebrides for written material in the Gaelic language ('Erse' or Irish as it was then known).

Isolated visits by curious strangers turned into a steady stream. Antiquarian research was pioneered by Richard Pococke, Bishop of Ossory, English by birth, Irish by adoption, with experience of travel in the Middle East to guide his steps. John Knox, a retired London bookseller, devoted his fortune and his pen to the improvement of the fisheries and manufactures of Scotland, particularly in the Highlands and Islands. A Welsh traveller and naturalist, Thomas Pennant, who found Scotland 'almost as little known to its southern brethren as Kamchatka', made the mistake of taking 'ribbons and other trifles' to the Hebrides when 'a few dozens of fish-hooks, or a few pecks of meal' would have made the natives happier. Sir Joseph Banks, fresh from a voyage round the world with Captain Cook and now on his way to Iceland, was tipped off about the geological wonders of Staffa, which he turned aside to visit and introduced to the world. Then in 1773 came Samuel Johnson, who left in forceful prose a graphic and authentic picture of life and manners as he saw them or learnt of them from those he met, while his friend and admirer James Boswell described their Hebridean hosts and companions as a foil to the personality and conversation of his hero.

All this produced a new vision of the Highlands in the public mind, and in a more tolerant atmosphere the repeal of the punitive post-1745 legislation was begun. In 1774 Simon Fraser had his family estates restored by Parliament after reminding them that he was the first who offered 'to set that example, which, in its consequences, proved advantageous to the State, by calling forth from a corner of the Kingdom many thousand soldiers, whose efforts to demonstrate their zeal and attachment to His Majesty's royal person and government contributed to the glory and success' of the last war. The new Fraser's Highlanders (71st Regiment) which he now raised for service in America was remarkable for having among his officers four other chiefs of clans (Cluny Macpherson, MacLeod, Cameron of Lochiel, and Mackintosh) and the sons of three others (Chisholm, Lamont and Colquhoun), besides other lairds and tacksmen, and recruiting was brisk even though some estates were still under forfeiture. The 71st won nearly all their battles and skirmishes, and it was not their fault that they became prisoners with the rest of Cornwallis's army at Yorktown.

With forgiveness in the Parliamentary air, an older grievance was also remedied when the Acts proscribing the name MacGregor were repealed in 1775. Here the petitioner ('for himself and many others') was Gregor Drum-

mond, the handsome soldier who had performed before the King's grandfather when the Black Watch uniform was first approved by George II. Now captain and adjutant of the Westminster Regiment of Militia, and with friends in high places, he explained how members of Clan Gregor like himself still passed under assumed names, although the Acts were now thought by many to be obsolete and the causes which produced them were 'now little known, and have long ago ceased'. Many MacGregors wished to resume 'the real name of their ancestors and families', but hesitated so long as there was 'the appearance

ABOVE Samuel Johnson, a Londoner of 63 (nearly twice the age of his companion), was taken more seriously. A sketch engraved by Thomas Trotter shows him in his travelling dress, described by Boswell as a 'very wide brown cloth greatcoat, with pockets which might have almost held the two volumes of his folio dictionary'

75

LEFT The repeal of the 'Diskilting Act' (as it was sometimes called) was widely welcomed in Scotland. The return of the jaunty garb excited much admiration – but a satirical English politician's print put forward one idea that the ban on it should be continued south of the Tweed

of a legal prohibition'. A Bill was quickly passed into law (with hardly a dissenting voice, 'though unfeelingly opposed by a narrow-minded nobleman'), and the name restored 172 years after the original ban by James VI.

As the clans were scattered and some of the chiefs and clansmen became men of influence far from the homes of their fathers, a feeling grew that some of the better features of the old ways of life were being lost. It was a desire to meet from time to time in the Highland garb, and to speak the tongue, listen to the music, recite the poetry, and observe the customs of their forefathers, that led to the founding in 1778 of the Highland Society of London. Lieut.-General Simon Fraser of Lovat was the first president, and John Mackenzie of the Temple, a lawyer with many contacts among landowners and merchants, was appointed secretary. The Gaelic language and literature were promoted by publication grants, prizes given for piping competitions, and Highland improvements and economic development fostered in a period marked by notable voluntary effort.

One of the first public objects taken up was the repeal of that obnoxious section in the Disarming Act which prohibited the wearing of Highland dress. The Act was twice renewed,

and it was still in force when Lord Hardwicke died in 1764, but portraits of the time and reports by travellers show that some people were venturing to wear the tartan before the ban was officially lifted. In 1782 a committee of the London society was appointed to approach the young Marquess of Graham (later third Duke of Montrose), a supporter of Pitt who sat in the Commons for an English constituency. On 17 June, Graham moved for leave to bring in a Bill, Lovat's half-brother and successor (Archibald Campbell Fraser) seconded, the repeal was agreed to and passed by the Commons on 21 June, approval by the Lords followed, and the royal assent was given on 1 July. A Gaelic proclamation said it must bring great joy to every Highlander, and Duncan *ban* Macintyre's 'song to the Highland garb' praised the son of the Graham chief for his action.

In some districts the dress had been completely abandoned and there was no wish to resume it. As Dr Johnson observed, 'the same poverty that made it difficult for them to change their clothing, hinders them now from changing it'. But one Argyllshire minister said it would take more than an Act of Parliament to make his people relinquish their ancient garb, and within a decade it was

Some of the gaiety, humour and costumes of the Scottish pastoral scene at the close of the eighteenth century were captured by the artist David Allan – a piper playing in a Highland cottage OPPOSITE, ABOVE and a Highland village dance with music provided by Neil Gow and his brother ABOVE

RIGHT One of the fishing villages in the Hebrides founded to help the local economy was sited at the head of Tobermory Bay in the Isle of Mull. It prospered, and some of the buildings shown in William Daniell's aquatint are still there

Tobermory, on the Isle of M...

reported to be widely worn in many Highland parishes. Startling news came in 1789 (the year after Prince Charles Edward died, and that in which the king's own recovery from illness was celebrated): three of the king's sons – the Prince of Wales (later George IV) and his brothers Frederick and William Henry, now all in their twenties – had been provided with complete Highland dresses, and instructed by Colonel John Small in the wearing of 'tartan plaid, philabeg, purse and other appendages'; the prince even wore the kilt at a masquerade in London.

This was not, however, the first time that a Hanoverian prince had worn the tartan. The Royal Company of Archers, which was to become the sovereign's bodyguard in Scotland, had adopted a predominantly red tartan as part of their uniform at the end of Queen Anne's reign. It seems that a miniature suit of this was made for the future George III, for the young prince is seen proudly wearing it in a charming group by the Swiss artist, Barthélémy du Pan, of the elder children of Frederick Prince of Wales. The date of the painting (1746) suggests that events in that critical year had not seriously prejudiced the royal family against all things with Scottish,

ABOVE Angus Munro, a piper in the 93rd Highlanders, served in the West Indies and competed at the Highland Society's Edinburgh competition in 1829 (which Mendelssohn attended) – this watercolour shows him with his wife, sweetheart or sister

and indeed Highland, associations.

In 1784, the forfeited estates were restored; Pitt's friend Dundas had long thought the return of the old chiefs might 'cherish and revive the spirits of the inhabitants of the North' and might stem the emigration. The restitution was subject to repayment of sums spent by government in clearing them of debt in the early years of forfeiture, and the £90,000 which they brought to the Exchequer was used for many purposes, and eventually for constructing roads and bridges.

Of the 12 estates now 'disannexed', as the official phrase had it, two went to colonels who had been officers in Fraser's Highlanders (Cluny and Lochgarry, the latter both in 1757 and 1775), and two more (Lochiel and Kinlochmoidart) to the sons of such officers; the heir of Struan also, forfeited (with intervals) since 1690, was a colonel in the king's service; in one case only did the forfeited laird himself live to be restored (Francis Farquharson of Monaltrie, who was 'out' in 1745 and was later pardoned). There had been many changes in the years since the estates were forfeited, and both chiefs and tenants had learned new ways: a form of 'commercial landlordism' had replaced the old paternal relationship, and fixed

Scott's *Lady of the Lake* was set in the area of loch and mountain LEFT known as the Trossachs, where Loch Katrine 'in all her length far winding lay, with promontory, creek and bay'. The stage success of *Rob Roy* produced many wonderful versions of Highland dress, such as T. J. Serle's in the title role BELOW; and West's theatrical prints featured the ordinary Highlander as well as the hero OPPOSITE, BELOW. *The*

Lord of the Isles introduced readers to the Hebrides, where in the Isle of Staffa 'Nature herself, it seems, would raise a minster to her Maker's praise', and to the mountains, lochs and caves of Skye; Daniell's view of Staffa RIGHT shows the busy scene off the great colonnade of basalt pillars near Fingal's Cave

MR SERLE as ROB ROY MACGREGOR

Published by M & M SKELT, 11 Swan St Minories London.

WEST'S. *New Miscellaneous Characters, in* ROB ROY.
In 6, Plates, Plate 1st Price 1d ½ Plain.

London, Published April 30, 1824, by W. West, at his Theatrical Print Warehouse,
57, Wych St. Strand.

For George IV's visit to Scotland, Turner came to Edinburgh and painted the march of the clans against the tremendous backdrop of the castle OPPOSITE, BELOW; and to see Sir William Curtis and the King, both wearing the kilt, was a gift for the caricaturists ABOVE; but Sir David Wilkie, who painted a state portrait OPPOSITE, TOP LEFT, thought His Majesty 'looked exceedingly well in tartan'. At least a decade earlier, Alasdair MacDonell of Glengarry had shown Raeburn his romantic idea of how a Highland chief should look OPPOSITE, TOP RIGHT

leases and regulations for good husbandry had been introduced by the Annexed Estates Commissioners.

The year which saw these estates restored also saw the founding of the Highland Society of Scotland. Argyll was president, but it was less wholly aristocratic than its London counterpart, and soon concentrated on the encouragement of agriculture as its principal function. It set out with the serious aim of inquiring into the condition of the region and its inhabitants, and how to improve them by establishing towns and villages, facilitating communications, advancing agriculture, extending the fisheries, and introducing useful trades and manufactures. The members were also to pay 'proper attention' to preserving the language, poetry and music of the Highlands, and they had their own bard, piper and professor of Gaelic.

The population in the Highlands was rising during the second half of the century, particularly in the west, but landowners were alarmed by the drift of tenants from their estates. It was hoped to find suitable work for some of them in the offshore fisheries, and a band of public-spirited individuals (supported by the Highland Society of London and headed by the Duke of Argyll) founded the fishing villages of Ullapool

in Wester Ross and Tobermory in Mull.

Less publicised than the sailing of emigrant ships was the 'steady and unplanned drift' to the Lowlands, where new villages were springing up in the 'fringe' areas with handloom weaving as the chief industry; in the great cotton mills at New Lanark, Blantyre and elsewhere, a large proportion of the workers came from the Highlands; and although the countryman then regarded large towns and cities as 'the graves of the human species', others went to Dundee, Perth and Edinburgh. Such places must have been a frightening contrast to the 'lone shielings' which they left behind them.

The army was another outlet for surplus population, and Lovat's example was soon followed. Six more Highland regiments were raised during the American war, including MacLeod's and Seaforth's Highlanders and a second battalion of the Black Watch. During the great struggle with France which began in 1793, Skye alone is said to have provided 10,000 soldiers, and from one hilltop in Morvern the minister could see the farms from which 60 officers had gone to fight Napoleon.

Now, 'divested of its sting' and no longer a danger to internal peace, the spirit of clanship could be encouraged. The chiefs obtained

commissions for their kinsfolk and cadets ('he that has nothing but sheep on his grounds could never expect a colonelcy'), and young men looked to the government for military preferment. By the end of the century the drain of men to the army was so serious in Badenoch and Strathspey that a total stop to 'the operations of husbandry' was feared; and in 1809, when enough men could no longer be found in the Highlands to fill the ranks of so many regiments (with two battalions in each), orders were given that six of them were no longer to be designated as Highland or to wear the Highland dress (four later got the tartan back, but not the kilt at first). Five Highland battalions now remained, but the 'native' element diminished year by year.

The wars against Napoleon, which gave rise to so many new regiments, also closed the gates of Europe to travellers of fashion. Just when a substitute was required, the poems and novels of Sir Walter Scott drew attention to scenes of beauty and romance nearer home. It was not long since mountain scenery was abhorred, but people now flocked to the 'land of brown heath and shaggy wood'. The Trossachs, which others had already praised, became more widely known and appreciated through *The Lady of the Lake* (1810); much to the

astonishment of those who lived there, every house and inn was crammed with visitors, anxious to see Loch Katrine and the combat scene at Coilantogle's ford where Roderick *dhu* assured FitzJames that 'these fertile plains, that soften'd vale, were once the birthright of the Gael'. Shortly before Waterloo, *The Lord of the Isles* sent tourists farther afield across the Hebridean seas to Loch Coruisk and the Cuillin Hills in Skye, and to Mull, Iona and Staffa. For those who missed the printed word, suitably adapted 'melodramas' followed promptly. A stage version of *Rob Roy* was produced in Edinburgh within a month of the novel's publication, London saw one three months later, and others proved a constant attraction over the next two decades.

Mention of the stage leads easily to the visit of George IV to Edinburgh in August 1822, when the romantic streak in the Scottish character which loves the pageantry that goes with royalty was given full play. No monarch had set foot in Scotland since Charles II left in 1651. King George spent two hectic weeks in his Scottish capital; he was 60 years old, and personally and politically unpopular, but he brought to his kingly role a zest and *bonhomie* which, under the tactful and enthusiastic stage-management of Sir Walter Scott, made

BELOW When the Scottish regalia were carried in procession from Edinburgh Castle during George IV's visit, Clan Gregor provided a guard of honour, and in Denis Dighton's watercolour they stand at the salute as the 'Honours of Scotland' are borne from the Crown Room
RIGHT A coatee of Murray of Atholl tartan was made to the order of the king's nephew, Sir Augustus Frederick d'Este, son of the Duke of Sussex.
OPPOSITE, BELOW At Dunkeld in 1842, Queen Victoria saw the sword dance performed to the music of the pipes

his visit an immense success. With only the briefest preparation, he carried through a strenuous programme of levees, courts, balls, a military review and civic banquet, and a state procession, which enabled him to be seen by thousands of his subjects and brought them, as well as the representatives of the ancient nobility and gentry who took all the most prominent parts, into the royal circle.

What made the most lasting impression during that fortnight of 'royal turmoil', apart from the King himself, was the extraordinary Celtic twist which Scott gave to the whole proceedings. Determined that 'Highlanders are what he will like most to see', he was urging clan chiefs less than a month before the King's arrival to bring 'half-a-dozen or half-a-score of clansmen' to Edinburgh for the occasion; Glengarry sent out a long list of the dress and accoutrements which a Highlander 'of decided respectability' should wear when waiting on the King (so greatly had the wearing of Highland dress apparently gone out of fashion); Colonel David Stewart of Garth, bespectacled and 'seamed all over with the scars of Egypt and Spain', who knew the story of the Highland clans and regiments as few others did, drilled and captained a detachment of the recently-formed Celtic Society and helped

Scott to adjust nice points of etiquette among the chiefs (who looked on Bannockburn as the valid precedent for fixing their own places); and an army clothier, George Hunter, met the sudden demand for tartans after scouring the Highlands in search of authentic specimens preserved in hut or castle. Seven bodies of clansmen, numbering some 300 all told, paraded during the visit, including MacGregors, Breadalbane Campbells, Sutherlands, Glengarry Macdonells, and Drummonds; chiefs of many other clans were there, vying with each other in the handsomeness of their equipages, and offers to send more contingents had to be declined.

At the first levee at Holyroodhouse His Majesty (not for the first time, as we know) wore the kilt, tartan coat, plaid and bonnet. It was one of two complete Highland outfits made for him by George Hunter, adjusted on the portly Hanoverian frame under the expert eye of Stewart of Garth, who pronounced him 'a vera pretty man'. The effect was somewhat lowered by Sir William Curtis, Lord Mayor of London (and a sea-biscuit manufacturer at Wapping), who appeared in the same attire – 'neither could refrain from smiling' when they met. Half the notables seem to have been in Highland dress for much of the visit, and Sir Walter so far forgot his Border ancestry as to wear trews of Campbell tartan (in memory of a great-grandmother). Argyll marched on foot at the head of a column of Highlanders the three miles between the city and Portobello sands for the military review (precedence among the clans had been determined beforehand by lot, and only the Glengarry men held aloof and joined the rest at Portobello). The clansmen were nearly cut off by the crowd, but the King himself ordered his commander-in-chief to arrange for the 'brave Highlanders' to march past him after the regular troops and volunteers, and admired their steady and soldier-like appearance.

OPPOSITE, ABOVE Highland games were arranged at Laggan in honour of Prince Albert's birthday when the Queen stayed at Ardverikie in 1847, and the royal couple watched the start of a hill race
OPPOSITE, BELOW The 'gillies' ball' became a feature of life at Balmoral Another of their early Highland holidays was spent at Blair Castle ABOVE, where the Duke of Atholl still has his own guard of Atholl Highlanders complete with pipers RIGHT

The most splendid occasion of all was the procession from Holyroodhouse to the castle when the Honours of Scotland – crown, sceptre and sword of state – were borne in full public view before the King (a ceremony deliberately recalling the old pre-Union 'riding of the Parliament', and repeated only once in 1953 for his successor Queen Elizabeth). The Clan Gregor were given pride of place in the escort, when the regalia were taken from and returned to the crown-room in the castle at the beginning and end of the visit – a fresh reminder, one can only suppose, that their long night of proscription was really over, and that they were once more looked on as loyal supporters of the crown. At the banquet in Parliament Hall, when the King called for a toast to 'the chieftains and clans of Scotland', it was Sir Evan MacGregor who replied with 'The Chief of Chiefs – the King'.

It is easy to laugh at the whole episode, and its ultra-Celtic element had many critics at the time. 'Sir Walter Scott has ridiculously made us appear to be a nation of Highlanders, and the bagpipe and the tartan are the order of the day.' A newspaper reported 'the invasion of the Celts', Lockhart wrote of the 'kilted rabble', and even Glengarry protested at the Celtic Society's 'burlesque' of the Highland character and dress. But the King himself was delighted, and without knowing it he had set the pattern (with the Celtic 'trimmings' modified) for more frequent royal visits to Scotland in the future. One of the immediate results was that a start was soon made with restoring the peerages forfeited by those who had supported Stuart against Hanover. But the visit had a lasting effect in identifying the Highlands with the rest of Scotland, and bringing them back into the main stream of Scottish life, and it was not long before the kilt was being hailed as the national garb.

George IV was never actually in the Highlands, but his niece Victoria developed an interest in the area which was gradual in growth but permanent in its effect. The Queen's first visit was in 1842, when she and Albert were only 23, and their reception by a gathering of the Atholl clans at a great encampment of 1000 Highlanders at Dunkeld was followed by a few days at Taymouth and Drummond Castle; in 1844 Blair Castle was lent to the royal couple for three weeks, and a pair of colours presented to the Atholl Highlanders a year later gave the Duke's ceremonial bodyguard a position enjoyed by no other 'private army' in the kingdom. In 1847 the royal yacht cruised through the Inner Hebrides, past Islay and Jura, round Mull to Staffa and

RIGHT Balmoral Castle: 'Every year my heart becomes more fixed in this dear Paradise, and so much more so now that *all* has become my dearest Albert's *own* creation, own work, own building, own laying out; and his great taste, and the impress of his dear hand, have been stamped everywhere' (Queen Victoria, 1856)

Iona, and up Loch Linnhe to Fort William; but the four weeks which the royal party spent at Ardverikie beside Loch Laggan were spoiled by 'dreadful' weather. Undaunted, the Queen heard of the dry and bracing air and beautiful scenery of Deeside, and next year she fell in love with Balmoral, where 'all seemed to breathe freedom and peace and to make one forget the world and its sad turmoils'. They bought the estate, demolished the old Gordon tower, and in 1855 completed the new castle nearby in the 'Scots baronial' style. Victoria and Albert revelled in the informality and adventure of their Highland home, and the sincerity of the Queen's love for the Highlands and admiration for the Highlanders breathes through every page of her journals, even when her way of expressing it makes one smile. The stamp of royal approval made others follow, and the extension of railways and opening regular shipping services on the west coast brought real local benefits as well as providing for the tourists who flocked to the north and west. The period of Highland isolation was ending, and towards the end of Queen Victoria's reign the special problems of the area began to receive special attention from the Government.

PAGES 92–93 One of the finest viewpoints in the basin of the Tay and its tributaries is the 'Queen's View' above Loch Tummel, where the royal party stopped for a picnic tea in 1866 but 'the fire would not burn and the kettle would not boil'
BELOW The Queen, her pony led by John Brown ('whom I have far the most confidence in'), crossing the ford of the Tarff in Glen Tilt, preceded by two pipers, and followed closely by Prince Albert and their attendants

Clan Tartans

Although there have been several references to Highland dress and tartan in previous chapters, not much has yet been said about colours or patterns, and nothing about any relationship which they may have had to individual clans. It will be convenient to notice these matters together here, and particularly to see what light can be thrown on the evolution of modern clan tartans.

The standard definition of tartan, or *breacan* as the Gaelic has it, is 'a kind of woollen cloth woven in stripes of various colours crossing at right angles so as to form a regular pattern'. Size or scale of pattern is unimportant – what matters is the proportion of the different colours, or *sett*, that is the relative width of the stripes or lines which go to make up the whole. It is customary (though there are exceptions) for the pattern to be symmetrical, the sett being the same for weft and warp, or in both directions of the cloth. This means that no two pure colours can lie next to each other, nor can there be a combination of more than two in any part of the web; but by having a number of such blends a much wider variety is achieved than the actual number of colours employed.

The weave used for tartan is the 'twill', in which the threads cross first over two, then under two producing the effect of a diagonal rib on the web. The thickness of the thread, and the shade of dye used to colour it, are left to the individual preference of weaver and wearer, which in modern times usually means that they are determined by the manufacturer, who is or should be guided by custom and good taste.

A love of bright colours has long been recognised as characteristic of the Highlander. Purple and blue are mentioned as favourites in the Hebrides at the close of the sixteenth century, and yellow and blue a century later; most tartans in current use have either green or red as the ground or dominant colour. It does not follow that these colours have always

been the easiest to obtain. Foreign dye-stuffs such as indigo and cochineal (for blue and red) have for long been imported, and could be supplemented by dyes obtained from native plants; yellow, the other component of green can be made from many sources. Where a muted colour was required, as for camouflage while hunting (or being hunted!), brown could be obtained from many lichens as well as plants. The old vegetable dyes had a mellow appearance which was at first lost when chemical dyes were introduced, but modern techniques have made it possible to recapture some of the old effect. The use of the adjective 'ancient' to denote this older type of colouring should not be allowed to delude the customer into thinking that the design of any tartan so described is more ancient than another.

Regarding patterns, an analysis of their structure can bring most of them within various groupings. This can be helpful in showing how each is made up and how it differs from others, but it can be shown that the simplest designs are not necessarily the oldest, and any attempt to associate similar patterns with a common blood relationship or location is liable to lead to wrong conclusions. One of the earliest writers on the subject, the Skyeman Martin Martin whose description of the Western Isles was published in 1703, tells us that the women were at great pains to give an exact pattern by means of a 'piece of wood' having the number of every thread of the stripe on it. As none of these 'pattern-sticks' has survived, some doubt has been thrown on their existence; others think they may have vanished during the proscription period, but the method was said to be still in use in 1830. Anyhow, they would be an effective aid to folk memory, and the practice of illustrating modern books on tartans by 'colour-strips' resembling a soldier's medal-ribbons adapts this idea, with the help of numerical tables to indicate the colour proportions or setts.

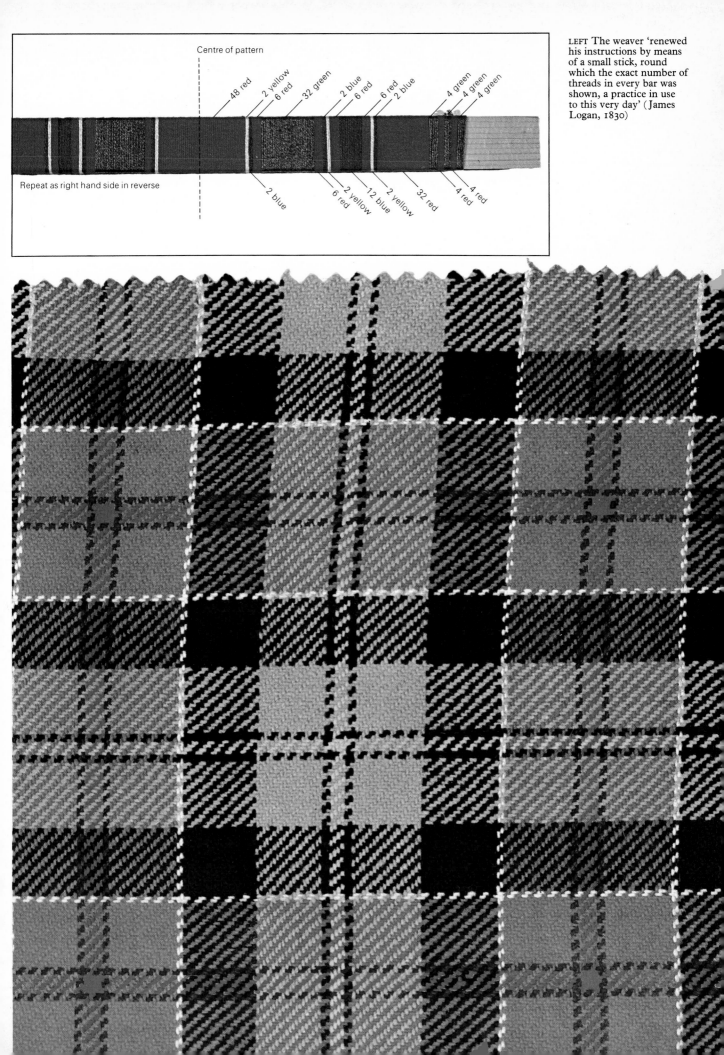

Centre of pattern

48 red
2 yellow
6 red
32 green
2 blue
6 red
6 red
2 blue
4 green
4 green
4 green

2 blue
6 red
2 yellow
12 blue
2 yellow
32 red
4 red
4 red
4 red

Repeat as right hand side in reverse

LEFT The weaver 'renewed his instructions by means of a small stick, round which the exact number of threads in every bar was shown, a practice in use to this very day' (James Logan, 1830)

From two of the earliest and best portraits showing Highland dress, we know that regularity and simplicity of pattern were not always regarded as essential. An oil painting by Michael Wright, dating from about 1660 but not certainly identified, depicts in life-size a chiefly figure wearing a belted plaid in several shades of brown and red, with black and crimson lines, on a 'cool buff ground', but the sett is not systematically squared and repeated as in modern tartans. About 50 years later, Richard Waitt's painting of Kenneth Sutherland, Lord Duffus shows a small and complicated pattern of which the colours are not easily distinguished.

There is some evidence that tartans were associated with different districts before any recognisable system of clan tartans had been established. Martin is again the clearest authority, although unfortunately he is lacking in detail: 'Every isle differs from each other in their fancy of making plaids as to the stripes in breadth and colour. This humour is as different throughout the mainland of the Highlands, in so far that they who have seen those places are able at first view of a man's plaid to guess the place of his residence.' Such district tartans were no doubt worn by members of the

RIGHT Michael Wright's portrait of a 'Highland Chieftain', which came from the Breadalbane collection, has been thought to represent more than one noble subject, but it is also suggested that the elaborate costume was worn by an actor playing the part of a Highland chief

OPPOSITE The portrait of Kenneth Sutherland, third Lord Duffus, a naval officer who joined the Jacobites in 1715, is by Richard Waitt, who also did a notable series of Grant portraits

BELOW Hugh Montgomerie, later twelfth earl of Eglinton, was an officer in his cousin and predecessor's 77th Highlanders in America, and also served in the Royal Scots
BELOW RIGHT Charles Campbell of Lochlane, near Crieff, an advocate and son of a judge, became a Sheriff after the 'Forty-Five'
OPPOSITE William Cumming, piper to the Laird of Grant, one of Richard Waitt's portraits formerly at Castle Grant

clans who lived in them, but the very fact that they were described as district and not clan tartans by an educated islander shows where the emphasis was laid in his day. It was the badge and not the tartan that distinguished the clan to which its wearer belonged, like the Frasers' yew and the Clan Donald's heath, which were known in Dundee's army in 1689.

But some 'group uniformity' of tartan was clearly gaining ground. The same bardic chronicler of the Killiecrankie campaign also wrote of Glengarry's men parading in tartan woven in triple stripes and his brother's in tartan with a red stripe, Maclean of Duart and his brother in flowing plaids with yellow stripes, and Macneil's plaid displaying as many colours as the rainbow. If that should be discounted as an example of poetic licence, the same does not apply to a 'hosting and hunting' order given by the Laird of Grant in 1704 to his tenants in Badenoch and Strathspey, and known from the records of his own courts, instructing them to have coats, trews and short hose of tartans of red and green sett, 'all broad springed'. Six years later, too, when the chief handed over the leadership of the clan to his son, the 'gentlemen and commons of his name' were summoned to appear in plaids of tartan of red and green. This suggests some wish for

uniformity, not only among the Grant tenantry, but also in the clan.

In a fine series of Grant portraits by Richard Waitt, no sett is repeated, except that the 'champion' and 'piper' of 1714 wear tartans consisting of red and grey stripes with fine black lines, and some yellow in the former. MacDonald and Murray portraits of a slightly later period show a similar variety of colour and pattern, bearing no relationship to the tartans later ascribed to these clans. It might be said of these portraits that the only thing they have in common is that the tartan undoubtedly gave scope to the artist and distinction to the subject, as in the painting of a Perthshire sheriff, Charles Campbell of Lochlane, painted about 1740 wearing the plaid separate from the 'little kilt'.

There are many references to 'Highland habit' and 'Highland clothes' in accounts of the '45, but little is known about the tartans then in use. All the more important, therefore, as evidence of what the ordinary Jacobite clansmen wore, is the lively painting by David Morier, George II's 'war artist', of an incident at Culloden for which the models were some of Cumberland's prisoners (who may of course have belonged to different clans). They are shown wearing jackets, waistcoats, belted

BELOW Major James Fraser
of Castle Leathers, 1723,
wearing tartan trews and a
large sporran of the same
material, was sent to
France by some of the
Fraser cadets to persuade
Simon Fraser to return
and command the clan in
1715

plaids, little kilts, trews and hose of varying patterns of tartan, no two men are dressed alike, and on the eight principal figures 17 different tartans can be distinguished, or 23 if we include the patterns of the hose. Here certainly is no sign that clan tartans were in use before the Highland dress was proscribed.

The 36-year ban on wearing tartan must have caused much of the traditional lore to be lost, and any natural development in its use halted. More than two-thirds of the generation who saw the ban imposed had died before it was lifted. Some recollection must have lingered among the women of the clans (to whom

incidentally the Act did not apply), but it was through the men of the Highland regiments that the Highland dress survived. The army was the only sphere in which it might legally be worn, and it was a privilege highly prized. Reference has already been made to the special military tartan which had been adopted; as new regiments were formed, narrow lines or stripes of different colours were added to the official sett in order to distinguish them. Thus MacLeod's Highlanders, raised in 1778 by John Mackenzie Lord MacLeod (son of the forfeited Earl of Cromarty, whose inheritance had embraced both names), had additional

buff and red lines – later changed to white and red, which was the variation also adopted by two regiments of Seaforth Highlanders. The Duke of Gordon chose a yellow stripe for his Fencible regiment raised in 1793, and a year later it passed to the regiment of the line known as the Gordon Highlanders. Both the Argyllshire and the Sutherland Highlanders, raised in 1794 and 1800, wore the military tartan without the addition of any lines, but the latter came to use a lighter shade (especially in the green groundwork) which still distinguishes their successors from the very dark shade worn by the Black Watch. The Cameron Highlanders, raised by Cameron of Erracht in 1793, departed completely from precedent by having a regimental tartan of their own, with green, blue and black as the dominant colours, and red and yellow lines, of which the origin has not been satisfactorily explained.

Nice distinctions are typical of military tailoring and more were to follow. The army kilt is so arranged that a particular or characteristic colour shall appear on the pleats in which it is folded. Thus the Black Watch kilt shows the blue stripe of the 'Government' tartan on 'piped' pleats, and the Argyll and Sutherland Highlanders show the green on a box pleat,

BELOW 'An Incident at Culloden', by David Morier, showing men of Barrell's Regiment attacking Jacobite forces, in which 'no two men are dressed alike'

RIGHT Highland Society of
London Certified Tartans,
begun in 1816. 'Many
genuine and well authenticated specimens of clan
and family tartans were
within a short time offered
for the acceptance of the
Society. These patterns
were made up into a hand-
some book which has
since remained in the
possession of the Society'
(Report, 1887)
Specimens from this col-
lection are illustrated on
pages 104–105

while the late Highland Light Infantry showed
the red line, the Queen's Own Highlanders
(who retain the Seaforth kilt) show the white
and the Gordon Highlanders the yellow. For
some reason, the scale of the basic military
tartan is not the same in all regiments, the old
Seaforth sett measuring 11 inches, and the
others seven. Such minutiae show how the
tartan can be 'regimented', and it is not sur-
prising that, when its wear became legal again
for civilians, they adopted some of the military
styles both in the wearing of the kilt and in the
dress that went with it.

Much of the tartan used by the army was

manufactured at Bannockburn, where one of
the busiest firms in the trade was William
Wilson & Son. In the decade after the ban was
raised their custom was largely for unnamed
or district setts, such as Aberdeen, Perth or
Crieff, but Gordon, MacDonald, Logan and
Bruce appear in 1792, Robertson in 1793, and
Chisholm and Stewart have been added by
1800. Some of these are explained by army
requirements, which also added the Mackenzie,
and an order for '30 yards 42^d Tartane of a
small pattern for childrens dresses' is a reminder
that in regimental schools the sons and
daughters of soldiers were clothed in kilts and

The samples in the image are labelled:

Small Durham · Small Argyle · 159 · Smallest 42°

Robin Hood 1/8 inch 82 ... ... · Clarke Tartan · Eglinton Tartan · Shepherds 6×6

Small Stewart · Wellington White ... · Large Gipsy · Small W. Duff 1861 ...

frocks of the regimental tartan in a small pattern or sett.

Those who believed that clan tartans had existed before proscription were puzzled by finding local uncertainty about what were the 'correct' patterns. Lieut.-Colonel Alexander Robertson of Struan, to whom the family estate had been restored as heir male, made inquiries about the 'Clandonachy tartan', only to find that the old men of the clan to whom he applied claimed to know the pattern, but that no two descriptions were exactly similar. As they were 'all very vulgar and gaudy', he decided to adopt the Atholl tartan, and he was still wearing it more than 20 years later, when (at the beginning of 1815) his clansman Andrew Robertson, miniature painter in London, was interesting himself in the subject. Colonel David Stewart of Garth, whose *Sketches of the Highlanders* was soon to become the classic on the clans and regiments, was enthusiastic over the idea (which Robertson seems to have originated) for preserving 'the different tartans, plaids and banners of the clans'. He urged the artist to persuade the Highland Society of London to ask each of the chiefs and heads of families to lodge an authenticated sample of his own tartan with the society before it was too

ABOVE While an attempt was being made to regularize 'clan tartans' the demand for tartan was so widespread that the manufacturers were kept busy inventing 'fancy' setts and new variations. A display of 12 hard tartans from an 1820 sample book of W. Wilson jun., Bannockburn, includes 'Robin Hood', 'Wellington White', 'smallest 42d', 'large gipsy' and 'small McDuff'

late. There could be no stronger proof that
such things would soon be forgotten than that
Struan, who though brought up in exile had
lived on his own estate for 30 years and always
wore the full Highland dress, 'does not properly
know what his own tartan is'.

Garth alerted all the chiefs within his reach –
Atholl, Menzies, Macnab, Chisholm and
Glengarry – and others too were anxious to
follow up the idea. Within three years the
Highland Society had the basis of a unique
collection of tartans, as authentic as the chiefs
could make it. Macalaster, Mackenzie and
Ogilvie, Chisholm, Colquhoun and Lamont
were among the earliest of a score and more of
samples submitted. Some, like Struan, no
doubt had to rely on doubtful evidence or
even personal fancy to 'fix' their sett, but
before long there were some unofficial ad-
visers. A mysterious pair who claimed descent
from Prince Charles Edward, John Hay Allan
and his brother Charles, were gathering
information on Lochaweside and elsewhere
about 'the *old* true Campbell sett', which the
duke himself was to adopt in place of the
42nd pattern; Cluny Macpherson and some
other chiefs also took the brothers' advice and
approved the design favoured by them. In
1819 a key pattern book in use by Wilsons
listed some 25 clan names, with an exact
thread count for each. The army clothier
George Hunter had been at work even before
he toured the Highlands collecting specimens
for George IV's visit, and later 'old Hunter'
was credited with having invented 'most of
the insignia for the Highland gentlemen of those
days', and even the clan tartans too. John
Wedderburn (later of Auchterhouse near
Dundee), secretary of the Highland Society of
London, was in Edinburgh in June 1822
'authenticating' a group of tartans which have
puzzled later commentators. Tartan-spotting
became something of a national pastime, and
other collectors included General Sir William

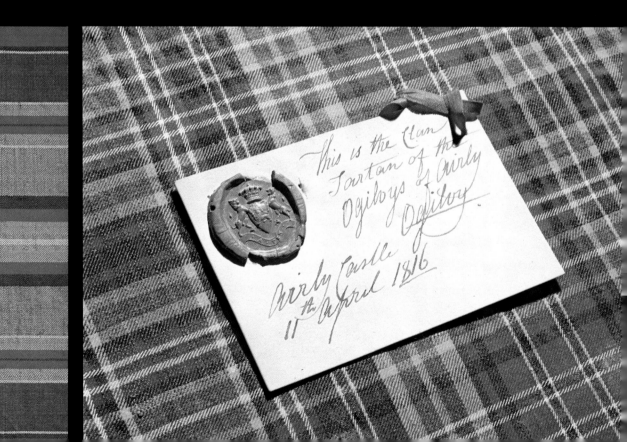

Cockburn of Cockburn, a member of the London society, and Sir Samuel Meyrick, an authority on armour.

It was also 'big business', as advertisements in the Edinburgh newspapers at the time of the king's visit show. It affected Paris fashions, and a transatlantic 'boom' followed. Offering to ship goods for the Wilsons, a Glasgow firm wrote: 'Tartans are much worn in America, and seen at all seasons, tho' best in the Fall; the patterns best adapted are large clan patterns for gentlemen's wear.' A New York order reported a fair demand in 1824, with a large-size Colquhoun as best of all, and MacDuff,

Bruce, Mackenzie and Glenorchy also good – but 'never mind whether they are any known tartan exactly – that is not cared for here'. Nearer home suppliers had to be more careful, and an order sent to a Dunkeld merchant was returned with the remark: 'I must be very particular with my *Atholl* Tartan – less exact pieces may do in places farther away than Dunkeld'. No wonder there was a demand for expert knowledge, and one old weaver at Bannockburn, noted for his intimate acquaintance with the various patterns, was dubbed 'the Lord Lyon of tartan heraldry'.

Where exactness was impossible, clear think-

BELOW A basic military or 'Government' tartan was adopted for the early Highland regiments in the British Army, with a pattern of broad green and blue bands and thinner black stripes. Lines of different colours were added by new regiments as they were raised – red and white for Seaforth, yellow for Gordon. Samples below show tartans supplied by a Scottish manufacturer for wear by the rank and file of five Highland regiments (Seaforth and Camerons are now united as the Queen's

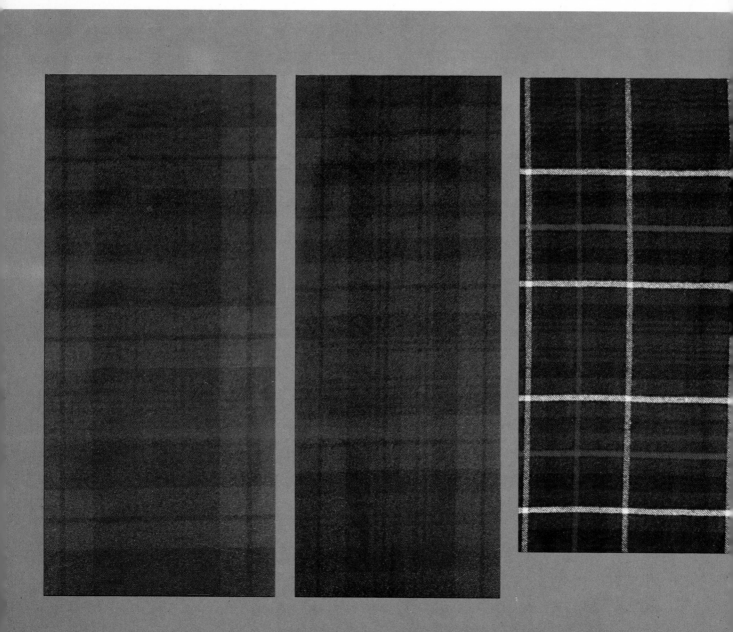

ARGYLL AND SUTHERLAND
HIGHLANDERS (OFFICERS)

BLACK WATCH AND
A & S H (OTHER RANKS)

SEAFORTH
HIGHLANDERS

Own Highlanders).
Officers' kilts were usually
made of finer material,
and here a darker shade
of colouring distinguishes
the Black Watch from the
Argyll and Sutherland
Highlanders who wore the
same sett. The Cameron
Highlanders' tartan was a
complete departure from
precedent

ing and systematic recording could clear up some of the confusion. Scott had always understood clan tartans to be 'of considerable antiquity', and he was sure he could show that they were in use 'a great many years before 1745'; but he was quite ready to admit that the distinction was probably neither so minute nor so unvariable as was generally supposed. 'I do not believe a word of the nonsense about every clan or name having a regular pattern which was undeviatingly adhered to,' he wrote in 1825. His friend Sir Thomas Dick Lauder, laird, antiquary and writer, lamented the 'woeful want of knowledge' then prevailing,

ridiculed the disputes over what were 'merely modern inventions for clothing regimental Highlanders', and declared (1829): 'Hardly does one of the clans now wear its tartan with its legitimate sets, stripes, and sprangues perfect in all their parts.'

The earliest attempt to publish detailed records of tartan patterns was made by James Logan in *The Scottish Gael*. The son of an Aberdeen merchant, he had studied law and art before becoming a miscellaneous writer in London (where he was secretary of the Highland Society for two or three years). He gathered his material the hard way, setting out

BLACK WATCH
(OFFICERS)

GORDON
HIGHLANDERS

CAMERON
HIGHLANDERS

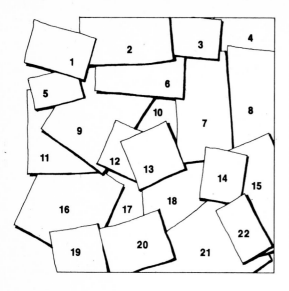

RIGHT The variety of colour and design in the tartans now associated with different clans is infinite and it is not the purpose of this book to list or identify them all. Green or red is usually the predominant colour, and clans which have both generally adopt the darker hue as a 'hunting' tartan for outdoor use, and the brighter one for 'dress' wear. The choice is, however, very much a matter for the wearer. Tartans in this composite picture, which does not always show the full sett, are associated with the clans and names as shown in the key LEFT

1. Mackintosh
2. Maclean
3. MacDonald
4. Fraser
5. Mackay
6. Buchanan
7. MacGregor
8. Campbell
9. Menzies
10. Macpherson
11. Robertson
12. MacKinnon
13. MacLeod
14. Chisholm
15. MacDougall
16. Ross
17. Cameron
18. Mackenzie
19. Grant
20. Lamont
21. Stewart
22. Macneil

on a pedestrian tour of Scotland in about 1826 'with staff in hand and knapsack on his shoulders'. His book appeared in 1831, and besides much other information it gave tables showing the pattern of 55 tartans, using a form of thread count in multiples of one-eighth of an inch. These tables included as many specimens as he could procure and authenticate, and he believed the list to be 'as correct as the most laborious personal investigations, and the able assistance of some valued friends, could make it'. Captain William Mackenzie of Gruinard, 72nd Regiment, who was one of those who helped him, had been 'out' with the Celtic Society in 1822, and his traditional knowledge of tartans provided a link with the pre-1745 period. Logan made a useful advance towards preserving established setts, but in spite of all his care the Wilsons regarded some of them as 'fictitious and fancy', and his scales are often open to different interpretations.

Logan's pioneer work was followed by an example of massive if oddly directed scholarship. Supposedly based on a sixteenth century manuscript was the famous *Vestiarium Scoticum* (1842), edited by John Sobieski Stuart (late Hay Allan) and illustrated by his brother Charles. Their original is generally thought to be an imposture, but many of the 75 clan tartans described have become firmly established in favour, and their author's wide reading and passionate sincerity are shown in their later *Costume of the Clans* (1845). Between these two works there appeared *The Clans of the Scottish Highlands*, with most of the text by James Logan and a series of 74 fine illustrations by R. R. McIan which, while their connection with particular clans is often

RIGHT Tartan is so adaptable that the association of different setts with specific names and communities is a continuing process. For example, most of the Canadian provinces have shown pride in their Scottish and Highland connections by adopting tartans of their own, as illustrated here

1. Ontario
2. Manitoba
3. British Columbia
4. Nova Scotia
5. New Brunswick
6. Prince Edward Island
7. Alberta
8. Newfoundland
9. Northwest Territories
10. Saskatchewan

ABOVE McIan's prints of the clans illustrate many types of Highland dress and the MacAlister (1), Lamont (2) and MacAulay (3) figures bring out the pathos, charm and strength of the Highlander. Donald Gregory, however, OPPOSITE, FAR RIGHT who became the painstaking and accurate historian of the West Highlands, thought a more elaborate garb was suitable for his appearance at the 1822 extravaganza

slender, show in a colourful and dramatic way the type of costume which may have been worn at various periods in the Highlands. Meanwhile, publishing clubs began to make accessible documents essential to a proper understanding of Highland history; the old bardic chronicles were verified from contemporary records by the research of Patrick Fraser Tytler and his cousin Donald Gregory, and W. Forbes Skene began his elaborate studies in Celtic language, literature and antiquities.

But Highland dress and history were far more than a matter of books. Open-air sport and athletics had been part and parcel of the old clan life, and traditional games fostered by local initiative and custom were given an added impetus by the Highland societies, even if something less spontaneous was occasionally imported if not imposed. The St Fillans Society promoted a full-scale event with piping, dancing and athletics; the Braemar gathering on Deeside was an indigenous growth long before it received royal encouragement; and up and down the Highlands popular support was given to many similar community efforts, in the success of which the wearing of Highland dress had an important part.

LEFT The Prince and Princess of Wales, later Edward VII and Queen Alexandra, are in the royal party watching an exhibition of Highland dancing from a knoll below Braemar Castle in 1864

RIGHT The Sobieski Stuart brothers, who claimed royal descent, lived in a romantic world of their own, as their self-portrait indicates, but had a considerable knowledge of Highland history and tradition

Clan Societies

Clan societies exist today as a sort of corporate personification of the clans – at once less than the whole clan, and yet more than any single member of it. Each one is likely to include most if not all of those who are conscious of and interested in being members of the clan whose name they bear.

In the days when nearly all the bearers of a clan surname were to be found in one region or district, united for mutual protection, and owing direct personal allegiance to their chief, the clan was literally itself a clan society. In fact, the purist might complain that the words are really tautological, and one society has

even recognised the fact (on the advice of an eminent Gaelic scholar) by making use of brackets in its title. The clans themselves are old, while the clan society is a comparatively modern institution, and by making a clear distinction between them we shall see them in better perspective.

The Buchanan Society, which recently celebrated its 250th anniversary, is the oldest clan society in Scotland. Instituted in Glasgow on 5 March 1725 under the name of 'The Buchanans Charity Society', it was granted a seal of cause or charter by the magistrates of the city in 1753 as a legal corporation 'of the

said name, the reputed septs, and branches thereof, owning themselves to be such, recorded in an historical and genealogical account of the same, by the late William Buchanan of Achmar'. The object of the founders was to assist the poor of the name and clan, to further the education of boys at school and university and their training for respectable trades, 'or the like pious uses', for which property was acquired and funds accumulated. Although not run on the same lines as most modern clan societies, the Buchanans have shown their 'clannishness' by various measures taken to perpetuate the memory of George Buchanan, the sixteenth century scholar and historian. The society, which has its own coat of arms, still flourishes, and the members continue to benefit others by their charitable work.

An early attempt was made to organise the Clan Chattan, which had become scattered. In 1727 an agreement was entered into between Lachlan Mackintosh of that Ilk and representatives of several tribes of Clan Chattan for the setting up of a fund to retain lawyers in Edinburgh, Inverness and Badenoch 'to watch and defend the interests of the clan against all who would seek the injury of any of the subscribers'; it was explained that 'by the members of the clan being so dispersed they are under the greatest disadvantage of any clan in Scotland in regard to their mutual defence'. There is nothing to show just what became of this attempt at co-operation, but it was still in existence three years later.

The Graham Charitable Society, founded in 1759 at a meeting of lairds, farmers, merchants and others of the name (perhaps with a sense of neighbourly rivalry with the Buchanans) has also survived. Its main object was to assist in the education and training of poor boys of the name and its connections, and to relieve the needy and it too received the sanction of the magistrates and town council of Glasgow (1770). It now devotes its activities to the payment of pensions either to members or to other persons of the name of Graham or their descendants, and very occasionally grants for educational purposes are given.

The next two societies show that the time of a clan's misfortune might be related to the formation of a clan society. Founded in Glasgow in 1806, the Clan Mackay Society (as reconstituted in 1888) has been described as 'the first of our clan societies' or (with more exactness) as 'probably the first genuine clan organisation ever formed in the South' – of Scotland, that is. The nineteenth century had hardly begun when the first 'clearances' took place in the Reay country, disturbing the old

order of things. Even before 1806, there had been partial removals from Lord Reay's estates when he reduced the leases of tenants, although it was not until later that the notorious 'Sutherland clearances' scattered the clan far and wide.

The object of 'McKay's Society' was 'to raise a fund for mutual help of each of us in the time of afflictive dispensations', and by observing certain rules and regulations they hoped to establish unity and good order amongst themselves. The men who drew these up were simple clansmen, whose names deserve to be held in honour. They were James McKay, undertaker (Preses or chairman); William McKay, grocer; John McKay, grocer; William McKay, vintner; Hugh McKay, vintner; and Hugh McKay, weaver (Clerk). The fourteen 'managers' appointed – again all Mackays – added the trades of cloth glazer, smith, plasterer and piper; the only appeal to clan tradition was a full-page black and white illustration of what were called 'The McKay's Arms'. Provision was made for members living outside Glasgow, and even outside Scotland. The society is said to have had a career of more than half a century, and may have helped to smooth the early path of city life for many Mackays from the Reay country in Sutherland.

BELOW Arms with supporters were granted by the Lord Lyon King of Arms to the Buchanan Society, the oldest clan society in Scotland, indicating its importance as a 'corporate clansman' in the social organisation of the kingdom

ROLL OF CLAN SOCIETIES

1725 The Buchanan Society
1727 Clan Chattan
1759 Graham Charitable Society
1806 McKay's Society (see 1888)
1822 Clan Gregor Society
1878 Clan Macnaughton Association (see 1952)
1888 Clan Mackay Society (1806)
1889 Clan Donald Society
1891 Clan Cameron Association
1891 Clan Campbell Society
1891 Clan Fergus(s)son Society
1891 Clan MacKinnon Society
1891 Clan MacLeod Society (see 1906)
1892 Clan Colquhoun Society
1892 Clan Maclean Association
1892 Clan Macmillan Society
1892 Menzies Clan Society (see 1958)
1893 Clan Donnachaidh Society
1895 Clan Lamont Society
1897 Clan Grant Society (see 1951)
1897 Clan Lindsay Society
1897 Clan Sutherland Society
1897 Clan MacDougall Society
1899 Stewart Society
1904 Clan Macnab Association
1906 Clan MacLeod Society (1891)
1908 Clan MacRae Society
1909 Clan Morrison Society
1912 Clan MacFarlane Society
1921 Clan Macneil Association
1923 Clan Macintyre Association
1931 The MacColl Society
1933 Clan Chattan Association
1936 MacCrimmon Society
1937 Clan Munro (Association)
1947 Clan Macpherson Association
1948 Clan Farquharson Society
1951 Clan Grant Society (1897)
1951 Clan Chisholm Society
1951 Clan Hay Society
1952 Clan Macnachtan Association (1878)
1952 Clan Rose Society
1958 Menzies Clan Society (1892)
1959 Clan Ross Association
1960 Clan Mackenzie Association
1960 Clan Fraser Association
1960 Clan MacLaren Society
1962 Clan Gunn Society

The MacGregors had suffered earlier than the Mackays, if not more harshly, but the penal statutes against them were repealed in 1775, and over 800 clansmen acknowledged a chief of their own name who was confirmed in the chief arms of Clan Gregor in 1795. Their prominent part in George IV's visit to Edinburgh in 1822 has already been mentioned, and later in the same year a number of gentlemen of the clan met together at the suggestion of their chief, and a society was formed 'for extending to the poor of the clan the blessings of a sound and Christian education, and more especially to select from amongst them, and encourage by pecuniary aid, or otherwise, such young men as give indications of talent or genius'. In the standing rules and regulations of the society it was laid down that 'no person who cannot satisfactorily prove that he belongs to the clan (by the father's side) and who does not bear or will not resume the name of the clan, viz., Macgregor, Gregorson, or Gregory, should be admissible as a candidate (for a bursary), or be eligible as a director'.

Although it arrived on the scene over 50 years later, a somewhat similar chain of circumstances is found as a background to the next clan society. The Macnaghtans' part in Dundee's Rising and subsequent events led to the loss of all their property in Scotland, and the Scottish line of the chief's family failed in 1773. In 1828, at the desire of upwards of 400 of the clan in Scotland, the head of a cadet branch in Northern Ireland was acknowledged as chief, and 50 years later a clan association was formed at a meeting in Edinburgh.

With these six societies, it seems to me, the early story of the movement comes to an end, and the modern phase begins. During the single decade of the 1890s, more than three times as many societies were formed as in the previous 160 years. There was a healthy spirit of rivalry among the clans, and the result was stated eloquently by the first president of the Clan Macmillan Society (the father of the late Lord Macmillan):- 'Such are the altered circumstances of the times, that we meet, not in secret, like the clans of olden times, beside a lonely mountain loch, with the mists gathering around it, or the moon shining in its mystic waters, afraid to have our plans known or our faces recognised, but under the full blaze of gas in a sumptuous hall in the heart of a populous city; and the cross of fire that has summoned us to this trysting place has been the advertisement sheet and the penny post'.

It is hard to explain just how it all started. It coincided with a new interest in Highland affairs, both in the cultural and the economic sphere. Inverness was a busy centre of literary and publishing activity, with men like Alexander Mackenzie and Charles Fraser-Mackintosh writing on the genealogical and social history of the clans as well as the current problems of land tenure and agriculture in the crofting areas. The Gaelic language – spoken, sung and written – was stimulated by the founding of An Comunn Gaidhealach with its annual 'Mod' (gathering) and competitions. The city of Glasgow had become a kind of expatriate Highland capital, and there Scotland was on show to the world at a great International Exhibition, which ran through six months of

1888, being opened by the Prince and Princess of Wales, attended by Queen Victoria, and visited by almost $5\frac{3}{4}$ million people. At this popular exhibition a proposal to reconstitute 'McKay's Society' as the Clan Mackay Society was first mooted, when John Mackay (of the 'Celtic Monthly') and another clansman were listening to a pipe band of the Argyll and Sutherland Highlanders led by a Mackay pipe-major and including two others of the clan.

New clan societies now crowded so fast upon one another that the development is best shown by a chronological list. It is also worth

BELOW The march of 1000 pipers along Edinburgh's Princes Street attracted huge crowds during the Festival of Britain celebrations in 1951

BELOW The Highland games held below Grandfather Mountain in North Carolina are designed to foster and restore interest in traditional dancing, piping, athletic achievement, and Gaelic culture

noting that the Clan Fraser was organised in Canada in 1894, Australia and New Zealand had clan society branches early in this century, and at least one association existed in America before it was established in Scotland. Most clan societies pass through periods of flourishing and decline, usually according to the amount of enthusiasm, imagination and leisure time that a few keen office-bearers can devote to them. They have often been criticised and even ridiculed, both for what they do and what they fail to do. One writer lamented that few have gone beyond the sphere of 'dinners, whist drives and bursaries', while another finds them lost 'in the realms of romanticism, of cult and ritual, mystical ancestor worship and the like – a joy to the tourist and folklorist, but a sorry end to a great tradition'. These complaints are not new – a Glasgow newspaper 80 years ago referred to 'the innumerable Highland clan societies that are swaggering in tartan, painfully acquiring the pronunciation of their respective battle-cries, and searching for chiefs', and to those 'who appear to think that the sole ambition of a modern clan should be to have a successful "cookie-shine" once a year'. Like most caricatures, this has an element of truth, and the very 'clannishness' which

makes one clan ignorant of what the others are doing has left the charge largely unanswered.

The cluster of societies formed or revived during the early 1950s is no accident. It can be mainly attributed to the Gathering of the Clans held in 1951 as part of Scotland's contribution to the Government-sponsored Festival of Britain. There had previously been some sporadic collaboration among clan societies, as for example in providing 'comforts' for men serving in the Forces during the two world wars, but the Council of Clan Societies formed to promote this gathering did much to bring them together. Some chiefships which

to such an extent that the '1000 pipers' made their way with difficulty through the crowds in Princes Street. The culminating event was the Highland Games and world pipe band contest on the Scottish Rugby Union's ground at Murrayfield attended by some 50,000 people; but what was specially memorable, and set the pattern for future events, was the scene behind the grandstand, where a score or so of clans – most of them organised into clan societies – had pitched their marquees, ranged facing each other round a great square. The organiser, Lieut.-Colonel George Malcolm of Poltalloch, inspired by accounts of the 'field

had been long in doubt had recently been determined by Lyon Court judgments on the right to 'undifferenced arms', and a Standing Council of Scottish Chiefs was formed to look after their interests.

The Gathering was held in Edinburgh for four days in August. There was a *ceilidh* or informal concert in the Usher Hall, when John Bannerman managed to impart a homely atmosphere with the audience participating, and nearly every tartan was represented at a brilliant Highland Ball in the Assembly Rooms. A massed parade of pipe bands through the streets of the city caught the public imagination

of the cloth of gold' which had dazzled all Europe in 1520, had imparted some of the splendour of medieval pageantry to the scene, for the banners of the chiefs floated above the tents, and the tartans of all the clans were mingled as the descendants of old friends and old foes alike met their kith and kin from all over the world. This impressive harmony had not been achieved without sacrifice, for some of the old clan rivalries had loomed menacingly over a projected 'march of the clans', to be led by the clan whose chief was the senior duke; one sensed a division like that between those who had supported Stuart and Hanover in

1745, until the chief promoters bowed to the inevitable and with the march replaced by an assembly of colour-parties everything went ahead more smoothly. The Festival brought an unusually large number of overseas visitors to Britain, and several clans also held rallies in their own clan countries.

The success of the 1951 gathering has already been repeated more than once, on a smaller scale and in association with some other event, at Inverness in 1960 and 1966, again in Edinburgh (Lauriston Castle) in 1962, and at the Royal Highland and Agricultural Society's showground at Ingliston, near Edinburgh, in 1972. The idea of the 'tented field' has been continued, and it seems to have inspired the organisers of other events, even overseas. At St Ann's, Cape Breton, where a Gaelic College was established in 1939, a succession of visits by clan chiefs to the Gaelic Mod and Highland Games was inaugurated by Dame Flora MacLeod of MacLeod in 1947. Scottish traditions have been fostered in the United States through events such as the Grandfather Mountain Highland games held at MacRae Meadow near Linville, North Carolina, in a region which an emigrant family from Kintail helped to develop.

Friendly co-operation among the clans on a world-wide scale has been spread by such great gatherings, but much of their success has been due to the enthusiasm of unpaid office-bearers of individual clan societies. Social, benevolent and educational activities, which still lie at the heart of many of them, are usually unspectacular, and the coming of the welfare state has made many changes necessary. Despite the impact of television, they have managed to encourage traditional entertainment in the form of song and story, the speaking of Gaelic, and the music of the harp and bagpipe. They have given a lead in the wearing of the tartan, which not so long ago had become the hallmark of an incomer to the Highlands, and a less formal style of life has rediscovered the kilt as an ideal garb for out-of-door activities. Above all, perhaps, is the two-way traffic of friendship, promoted by the clan societies, which has forged new links of understanding between clansfolk at home and beyond the seas.

Clan societies have a natural desire to perpetuate the history and traditions of their clans, and many have done so in the form of books, periodicals and (more recently) recordings. The Clan Mackay Society led the way in the 1890s by publishing a number of historical works, the Clan Maclean Association sponsored a collection of their clan music, and the Clan

ABOVE Clan societies have helped to preserve and make known the story of their ancestors and record present-day events and achievements by the publication of books and periodicals. These magazines circulate among members throughout the world and find a permanent place in various libraries

OPPOSITE, ABOVE Kisimul Castle was restored by Macneil of Barra between 1938–60 from a ruined shell to a habitable home OPPOSITE, BELOW This group at Moy Hall includes The Mackintosh and his lady, McBain of McBain, Major Shaw of Tordarroch, and Captain Farquharson of Invercauld, and a McIntosh from U.S.A. who is a chief of the Creek Indians

Lamont Society printed two papers on the clan tartan. Others have helped in the collection of material, and provided a market for the finished product. Standards of quality and presentation have of course varied: and while some writers have known too little of Highland history beyond their own clan, the particular viewpoint has often been justified as a corrective to other accounts. 'We, as a clan, desire neither to be unnecessarily praised nor unduly traduced,' said a MacFarlane writer, 'but owing to the tardy appearance of this work our "unfriends" have had a long rope. The taunts "cattle thieves", "name your chief", "broken clan", and the like are ill to brook, yet what was to be expected when the origin of these was the tainted source of the historian of the ancient enemy, paid to produce a history of the Clan Colquhoun?' One of the most sumptuous and well-authenticated of clan histories, *The Lamont Clan*, by Hector McKechnie, was initiated by two American members who were so impressed with the good fellowship and ideals of the clan society that they offered to find four-fifths of the sum required to publish a full history of the clan, provided the society would raise the balance and members would contribute any traditional or other knowledge that they possessed.

Their historian found much of his material in the *Clan Lamont Journal*, which since 1912 had combined an interest in past history with a record of current activities. Some clan periodicals have had a brief existence, like the MacDougalls' well-named *Galley of Lorn* which expired on the outbreak of war in 1914, while others – *Clan Chattan* (founded 1934), *Clan MacLeod Magazine* (1935), the Macphersons' *Creag Dhubh* (1949), and *Clan Donnachaidh Annual* (1951) – have had a long run and still appear regularly. *Clan Munro Magazine*, after producing ten issues, was able to rejoice in the birth of two daughter publications, *Munro Eagle* and *Munro Beacon*, in the United States and Canada. In addition to publications, every clan society maintains the feeling of kinship through correspondence: a healthy interest in ancestry, for instance, prompts many genealogical inquiries, some of which are of purely personal interest and significance, while others throw light on the structure and history of the clan.

In an even more practical way, some societies have ensured the preservation of important clan relics. The *Bratach Bhan* or white banner of the Mackays, once celebrated in song and story, was secured for the Clan Mackay Society, and is on exhibition at the National Museum of Antiquities in Edinburgh.

The Clan Macpherson Association opened their own museum at Newtonmore in 1952, and their 'green banner' and 'black chanter', and many of the Cluny papers (dispersed since the chiefs' estate was sold) are in their possession. The first purpose-built Scottish clan museum is the home of the Clan Donnachaidh Association at Bruar Falls, where a variety of objects, pictures and documents tell the story of the clan, the country and the society, and the life and achievements of individual clansmen and clanswomen.

Economic and social changes, hastened by two world wars, led to the break-up of great landed estates and the sale or abandonment of many historic houses. This made it all the more appropriate that some societies should cherish the dream of owning part of the old clan territory, although this is not a role which a body with such scattered membership can readily undertake. Two small islands, Clairinch in Loch Lomond and Inchmahome in the Lake of Menteith, were bequeathed to the Buchanan Society and the Stewart Society – the former is now a bird sanctuary, and a thirteenth-century priory on the latter is in Government care as a national monument. The Lamonts, who had for many years wanted to secure a footing in Cowal, found themselves unable to accept a gift of the Knockdow estate for financial reasons. The Menzies Clan Society bought the ancient home of their chiefs, Castle Menzies near Weem, in 1957, and it has attracted a substantial Government grant for restoration as a fine example of 16/17th-century Scottish domestic architecture. On an even larger scale is the formation of the Clan Donald Lands Trust (of which all members of Clan Donald Societies throughout the world are members) in an attempt to save the 40,000-acre MacDonald estate in Skye from falling into the hands of strangers, and preserve it for the enjoyment of the clan.

The restoration of clan strongholds is nothing new, although it is unusual for a clan society to tackle it. Duart Castle in Mull was rebuilt by the late Sir Fitzroy Maclean, who lived to pass his 102nd birthday within its walls; Eilean Donan in Wester Ross was restored by a descendant of its last MacRae constable, and opened in 1932 at a great gathering of Clan MacRae; and Kisimul, built on a rock in Castlebay, Isle of Barra, became the home of Macneil in 1960 after a lifetime's planning and practical work. The Historic Buildings Council for Scotland, soon after it was set up as a Government agency in 1953, recognised the importance of preserving such

ABOVE Memorial stone on Cannich brae above the house of Comar, the principal place in the barony granted to the Chisholm chief in 1538
BELOW Clans are family affairs – Captain Patrick Munro of Foulis welcomes members of the Clan Munro (Association) at a gathering in Ross-shire, when his eldest son and heir Hector (left) received coming-of-age gifts from the clan

OPPOSITE, ABOVE MacLeods have held a 'Clan Parliament' at Dunvegan Castle in Skye at regular intervals since 1956. During the seventh of these, in 1974, this picture was taken of 180 members of the Associated Clan MacLeod Societies from all parts of the world, including Canada, U.S.A., Australia and New Zealand

OPPOSITE, BELOW LEFT John MacFadyen, a well-known piper, plays a pibroch beside the MacCrimmon cairn at Borreraig; Seton Gordon, author and piping expert, is seen beyond
OPPOSITE, BELOW RIGHT Dame Flora MacLeod of MacLeod arrives at Borreraig by boat from Dunvegan Castle

places, known to and revered by Scots throughout the world, and building grants have been given for Dunollie House, Dunvegan, Foulis, Kisimul, Blair and Castle Menzies.

In Scotland practically every place has its link with history, and these old castles attract the general tourist as well as the pilgrim in search of the cradle of his race. At various spots of clan significance 'historic markers' have been placed by clan societies. As far back as 1881 the Buchanan Society became permanent custodians of the monument to the historian and scholar George Buchanan at Killearn. The Clan MacRae Society erected a cairn at Sheriffmuir, where many of their clan fell in 1715. Near the site above Loch Dunvegan in Skye where the MacCrimmons had their college of piping, the Borreraig cairn was built by the Clan MacLeod Society and unveiled by their chief in 1932. The Stewart Society placed several clan memorials in Appin, and a statue of General Stewart of Garth at Fortingall, and also presented entrance gates for a park in Bathgate as a memorial to the ancestor of the Royal House of Stewart. Acting on the suggestion of an Australian member, the Clan Chisholm Society marked the spot in Glen Cannich (now submerged by the waters of Loch Mullardoch) where according to tradition The Chisholm used to take counsel with his clansmen, and other commemorative stones have been placed at various points in the old clan country. On a hillside overlooking Loch Ness the American-born chief in 1960 formed the unique 'Clan McBain Memory Park' on a plot of heather-clad moorland which once formed part of his ancestors' lands of Kinchyle.

Most of what the clan societies are doing is traditional, based on ties of sentiment and loyalty, but the more adaptable have found new forms for such activities. The Clan MacLeod Society, growing in strength as a result of 'MacLeod Days' at Dunvegan and their chief Dame Flora's series of world tours to meet her clansfolk, held their first 'clan parliament' at Dunvegan in 1956, and every three years since then the Associated Clan MacLeod Societies have met in formal and informal conclave. In tune with modern research, the pursuit of purely genealogical data has been widened to embrace social and economic, demographic and archaeological studies of clans and clan areas. While unashamedly drawing much of its inspiration from the past, the movement has steadily become more forward-looking. Since 1964 the Clan Chattan Association has thrice played host to a Highland Industries Exhibition, combined by Lieut.-Commander Lachlan

Mackintosh of Mackintosh with a clan gathering at Moy in order to focus attention on the products and problems of public and private enterprise in the area.

It is a practical reminder that even in the Highlands history does not stand still. A nostalgic notion of the past should not blind us to the changes which are taking place around us and are projected for the future. Some of the finest holiday and recreation areas in Britain are to be found north of the 'Highland line'. There is much there that should be preserved unspoilt, but much also that could be improved. In remembering the clans, and striving to retain something of their old spirit of comradeship, their pride of family and love of country, it would do no service to their memory to create an empty wilderness without people, or even a region of fine scenery whose few inhabitants were wholly dependent on visitors and tourists for a livelihood. Change and development there must be, without destroying all the beauty of the Highlands; but the home of the clans has its own aura of glamour and romance, and in the eyes of many who know it their human story is not the least of its attractions.

Highland games are held annually at Glenfinnan, near the spot where the standard was raised in 1745 and here piping and athletic events are enjoyed by local people and visitors ABOVE March to the games field, with Colonel Sir Donald Cameron of Lochiel and Seton Gordon leading the march behind the pipers; BELOW hills and clouds for a typical Highland background to a piping competitor at Glenfinnan games

Index

Note: This index contains references to both text and captions to illustrations. Clans and clan chiefs are listed together in alphabetical order under the heading Clans, Clan system. Individuals bearing a clan surname are listed in normal alphabetical order.

Acknowledgments

The author would like to express his thanks to the friends and clan societies who were so helpful in providing photographic material.
The author and publishers wish to express their gratitude for the kind permission to reproduce the following photographs; photographers of works in collections are in brackets.

Reproduced by gracious permission of Her Majesty The Queen 56–7, 61 above left, 85 above left, 88 below, 90–1, 100–1; Sample supplied by Gordon & Sons, Edinburgh 95 below, 106–7; Barnaby's Picture Library 65; Bibliotheek van de Rijksuniversiteit te Gent 24 right; The Black Watch Museum, Perth (Dr. W. H. Findlay) 73 above right; British Museum (John R. Freeman) 16–17, 29 above right, 38, 45, 58 above, 59 above, 60 above, 61 below, 68–9, 75, 84, 112 above right and right, 113 above left; Courtesy of the Clan Buchanan Society (Angelo Hornak) 115; Courtesy of The Marquess of Bute (Rupert Roddam) 46 above left; Canadian War Museum 73 below; Canongate Museum, Edinburgh (Angelo Hornak) 76 below, 87 above, 103; Dr. Fanny B. Chisholm 121 below, 122 below; Collection of the Coldstream Guards (Michael Holford) 70–1; Colour Library International 22–3; Confederation Life Insurance Company 63 above; Masters and Fellows of Corpus Christie College 10 above; Court of the Lord Lyon 12 above right; Courtesy of the Clan Donnachaidh Society (Angelo Hornak) 116 above; Anne-Marie Ehrlich 54–5, 67 below; Courtesy of the Trustees of the late Mrs. M. Sharpe Erskine, Dunimarle Castle, Culross, Fife/National Galleries of Scotland 76 above, 76–7; Mary Evans Picture Library 88 above,

112 below, 114; Courtesy of The Hon. Hugh Fraser 113 below; Lt. Col. Aubrey Gibbon (Angelo Hornak) 79; Glasgow Art Gallery 43 below; Samples supplied by Thomas Gordon and Sons, Glasgow (Angelo Hornak) 106, 107; Robert Harding Associates 20 above centre; Leslie F. Heggie, Victoria, Australia 123 below; The Highland Society of London (Angelo Hornak) 102, 104–5; J. Davidson Kelly 19 below; A. F. Kersting 26–7, 92–3; Keystone Press Agency 89 below; Dr. W. D. Lamont 12 below right, 20 below, 27 below, 29 below; Mansell Collection 87; Roberto Matassa 20 below centre, 44 right, 53 above, 82–3; Mitchell Library, Sydney, Australia 89 below; Hugh Morton, North Carolina 4–5, 118; Courtesy of Dr. Jean Munro (Angelo Hornak) 95 above; Courtesy of R. W. Munro (Angelo Hornak) endpapers, 120; Col. Sir Gregor MacGregor of MacGregor (Tom Scott) front jacket, 86, 113 above right; Associated Clan MacLeod Societies/Skye Agencies 123 above; Dr. Herbert P. MacNeal, New Jersey 20 above; Ian R. Macneil of Barra 117, 121 above; Samples supplied by Hugh Macpherson (Scotland) Ltd., Edinburgh (Angelo Hornak) 108–9, 110–11; National Gallery of Scotland (Tom Scott) 41 below, 85 above right; National Library of Scotland 11 above, 66; National Library of Wales

59 below; National Museum of Antiquities of Scotland (Angelo Hornak) 1, 25, 32 above, 34–5, 43 above, 71 above left, 99; National Trust for Scotland 32 below, 33, 46 below; Jim Nicholson 53 below; Courtesy of Sir David Ogilvy/National Library of Scotland 36; Andrew Paton 124–5; Picturepoint 10 below, 18; Don Pottinger 13, 34; Royal Commission on the Ancient and Historical Monuments of Scotland 19 above, 24 left, 28, 29 left; Scottish National Portrait Gallery 27 above, 31, 37, 50 left, 62 above, 96, 97, 98, 100, (Tom Scott) 39, 51, 52; Scottish Tourist Board 11 below (J. Pugh) 12 left, 119, Scottish United Services Museum (Tom Scott) 47 above, 47 below, 48–9, 50 right, 71 right, 72, 73 above right; Sotheby's 9 above, 63 below; Courtesy of the Right Honourable The Earl of Southesk Scottish National Portrait Gallery 40; Spectrum Colour Library 2–3, 17, 42, 46 above right, 64 above and below, 80 left; Sunderland Museum and Art Gallery 62 below; Tate Gallery, London (Rodney Todd White) 85 below; J. C. Tait 122 above; Courtesy of United Services and Royal Aero Club (Angelo Hornak) 44 left; Victoria and Albert Museum (John R. Freeman) 74, 78–9, 80 right, 81 above, 81 below; James Weir 8–9, 41 above, 78 above, 89 above; ZEFA (J. Pugh) 14–15, 90 above.